SKY BLUE H...
VOLUME ...

BY GRAHAM SMITH
& NEVILLE HADSLEY

First Published in 2006
by Elephant Books
c/o **4 Newgate Court, Paradise St, Coventry, CV1 2RU**
ISBN 10: 0-9552642-0-0   ISBN 13: 978-0-9552642-0-7

www.skyblueheaven.co.uk

© Graham Smith & Neville Hadsley

Printed by Senik Print, Coventry. Tel 024 7622 4344
Cover by Phil Dee of Alison Philip Design. Tel 01788 546565

THANKS TO:

Peter Hall for his cricket knowledge and more, Kev Monks, Dennis Strudwick, Derek Smith, Berni Smith, Anne Smith, Shawry, Lynne Shepherdson for the proof-reading, Stuart for his help with the printing, Phil for the cover, Coventry Central Library, and the Coventry Evening Telegraph.

ABOUT THE AUTHORS:

Graham Smith *became a fan of Coventry City when he was taken to the "Midlands Match of the Century" against Wolverhampton Wanderers in April 1967. His father, a BBC producer, had just completed a documentary about the Sky Blues manager Jimmy Hill. With a record 51,000-plus attendance it was an unforgettable first match for an 11-year-old, sitting on the grass on the edge of the pitch. Graham worked as a news cameraman for Midlands Today, 1972-78, then moved to Leeds and worked for BBC North. He worked for 20 years as a documentary cameraman for the BBC, ITV and C4 on a wide variety of subjects. As a writer he has contributed articles to magazines on beer and canals and a chapter to the book "Ernie Hunt's Sideburns. "Sky Blue Heaven" was his first book. His other interests include skiing, cycling and the cinema. He speaks conversational French. He divides his time between his canal narrow boat and house in Spain. He is married to Berni, a Business Travel manager. His favourite all-time Coventry City players are Ernie Hunt and Mick Ferguson.*

Neville Hadsley *was born in Coventry in 1959 and can just about remember attending Highfield Road to support the Sky Blues in the late 1960s. His most vivid early memory is seeing Coventry City beat Bayern Munich in the Fairs Cup in November 1970. He has been a City supporter ever since. In 1998, he founded the Sky Blues fanzine Gary Mabbutt's Knee and established the Sky Blues fansite GMKonline.com in 2000. He edited both until 'retiring' from the world of fanzines in August 2005. He has written on Coventry City for numerous publications, including When Saturday Comes, The Coventry Evening Telegraph, The Birmingham Post, The Sunday Mercury, The Guardian and The Observer. He lives with his partner Lynne and their son Oscar.*

Also Available from the same authors
Sky Blue Heaven – An Encyclopedia of Coventry City FC
ISBN 1 872204 90 2

INTRODUCTION

If you are the lucky owner of a copy of **Sky Blue Heaven An Encyclopedia of Coventry City FC,** *you may be thinking this is a reprint of the same book, but it isn't.*

Equally, if you have only ever seen this book – **Sky Blue Heaven Volume II** *– then you will be wondering how on earth an encyclopedia of Coventry City FC can miss out on Jimmy Hill, Steve Ogrizovic and the 1987 FA Cup Final. The simple answer is: The two books go together. Almost everything in* **Volume II** *is completely new.*

What isn't new is that the same quirky, off-the-ball humour for which Sky Blue Heaven became famous is to be found in these pages, too.

This book was inspired by the shattering realisation that Sky Blue Heaven *had missed out on a key figure in Coventry City history – Brian Roberts. That got us thinking. And a few beers later, we concluded that, with our first effort, the surface of Planet Sky Blue had merely been scratched.*

The more we looked, the more we found other grievous omissions and amazing trivia that somehow had escaped our orbit. For example, in our first volume, we thought we had written the definitive treatise on Monty Python's

Flying Circus and their apparent obsession with Coventry City FC. But no. We found more.

And so, Sky Blue Heaven Volume II *was born. Included within these covers are the stories of some of the greatest figures in Coventry City's history, who we somehow missed out first time. There is also an improved and generous helping of the facts and figures that every Sky Blues supporter will want to know. Who scored City's quickest-ever goal? Who are the top 20 goalscorers of all time? Which player was sent off more than any other?*

Plastic pitches, shirt sponsors, penalty shoot-outs, debutant scorers, unsung heroes, nicknames, it's all here – a veritable Sky Blue universe.

Together with Volume I, Sky Blue Heaven Volume II *provides plenty of* I-never-knew-that-ness. *While researching and writing it we were constantly surprised by the things we were unearthing. It's been a pleasure writing, this book – we hope you enjoy reading it.*

In the mean time, we raise a glass to Brian Roberts. Here's to you Harry; you made it all possible.

GS &NH

STATS AND FACTS

LEAGUE CUP

The generic term for the cup contested by League Clubs.
The sponsors names for this trophy are:

1961-81	No Sponsor
1982-86	Milk Cup
1987-90	Littlewoods Cup
1991-92	Rumbelows Cup
1993-98	Coca-Cola Cup
1999-03	Worthington Cup
2004-	Carling Cup

LEAGUE NAMES

The following are the official titles for the leagues that are given general or popular names in the book.

1967-84	League Division 1	Top Division
1984-86	Canon League Division 1	Top Division
1986-87	Today League Division 1	Top Division
1987-92	Barclays League Division 1	Top Division
1992-93	FA Premier League	Top Division
1993-01	FA Carling Premiership	Top Division
2001-04	Nationwide League Division1	Second Division
2004-05	Coca-Cola Championship	Second Division

ABBREVIATIONS

apps. appearances.
Att. attendances.
o.g. own goal.
aet after extra time.

WHAT'S IN AND WHAT'S OUT

Unless stated, otherwise, statistics are from 1919 when Coventry City became a league club, until the end of the 2004-05 season. Games played during the Second World War are not included. Although there are separate sections on Friendlies, Testimonials and Overseas Games, they are not part of any statistical table or totals for historical record. The same applies to optional cups such as the Southern Professional Floodlit Cup, Texaco Cup, Full Members Cup, Simod Trophy, ZDS Cup.

Willie Carr, whose goal helped City to victory in a rearranged fixture in 1972

ABANDONED GAMES

Extreme weather and technical failure have caused Coventry City matches to be abandoned 13 times, but possibly never more frustratingly than on the very first occasion, in 1903. City were playing Halesowen in the Birmingham & District league and the game was just eight minutes away from a conclusion when the referee decided to call it off for fog and force the match to be replayed.

The score was 0-0 at the time and it remained so in the rearranged fixture, meaning that the two teams battled out almost three hours of football without a goal.

Fog, snow and even heavy rain have all caused games to finish early over the years. Floodlight failures have also struck twice, once at Highfield Road in 1956 and once in 1972 at Portman Road.

Perhaps the most serendipitous abandonment that City ever experienced was at Highfield Road in March 1972 against Sheffield United when snow intervened just after the hour. One suspects that the majority of the 16,408 in attendance went home happy as the Sky Blues were losing 2-0 at the time. The smiles were even broader, no doubt, when City won the rearranged fixture 3-2. Bobby Graham, Willie Carr and Ernie Machin were City's scorers.

In most cases though, as anyone who has ever attended an abandoned game will testify, the feeling when the referee ends matters prematurely, is one of deep frustration.

Happily such instances are rare these days. Milder winters and better-protected pitches in better stadiums have almost eradicated the curiosity that is the abandoned game. Not that stops City fans praying for rain, snow or hail in biblical proportions from time to time. Anyhow, below is a complete list of abandoned games involving Coventry City:

v Halesowen (h) Nov. 28, 1903. *ab. 82 mins. 3-1 Fog.* Re-arranged result D 0-0.
v Stafford R. (h) Dec. 2, 1905. *ab. 60 mins. 1-1 Rain.* Re-arranged result W 3-0.
v Bilston (a) FA Cup. Oct. 19, 1907. Att. 4,000. *ab. 70 mins. 2-1 Hailstorm.* Re-arranged result W 2-1.
v Reading (a) Mar. 6, 1909. *ab. 45 mins. 0-1 Rain.* Re-arranged result W 1-0.
v Northampton T. (a) Oct. 1, 1910. *ab. 51 mins. 0-0 Bad Light.* Re-arranged result L 1-4.
v Southampton (h) Dec. 4, 1937. Att. 10,000 *ab. 45 mins.
1-0 Snow.* Re-arranged result W 2-0.
v Sheffield W. (h) Nov. 19, 1949. Att. 17,541. *ab. 63 mins.
1-0 Fog.* Re-arranged result W 3-0.
v Southend U. (h) Mar. 26, 1955. Att. 4,100. *ab. 68 mins.
3-1 Heavy Rain.* Re-arranged result L 1-4.
v. Crystal Palace (h) Dec. 22, 1956. Att. 8,226. *ab. 51 mins. 0-0 - Floodlights.* Re-arranged result 3-3.
v. Newport C. (a) Dec. 25, 1956. Att. 7,500. *ab. 71 mins. 0-0 - Blizzard.* Re-arranged result L 0-3.
v. Colchester U. (h) Dec. 22, 1962.
Att. 11,803. *ab. 45 mins. 2-0 Fog.* Re-arranged result 2-2
v Sheffield U. (h) Mar. 4, 1972. Att. 16,408. *ab. 62 minutes 0-2 - Snow.* Re-arranged result W 3-2.
v Ipswich Town (a) Nov. 25, 1972. Att. 19,336. *ab. 61 mins. 1-0 - Floodlights.* Re-arranged result L 0-2.
Coventry City score appears first.See also: Friendlies at Highfield Road - Mid Season, v. San Lorenzo) Testimonials, v. Millwall; International Games Staged.

APPEARANCES
Modern football has transformed the loyal, one-club player into an endangered species, so it seems inconceivable in the current climate that anyone will ever get close to breaking Steve Ogrizovic's magnificent record of 601 games for Coventry City. Even allowing for the fact that goalkeepers play longer than outfield players, George Curtis' record of 538 games seems fairly safe.

Richard Shaw, alone amongst the most recent crop of Coventry City players, has broken into the top ten, but the next one to achieve that feat may be many years off.

• Steve Ogrizovic holds the record for most appearances in the FA Cup, 34. George Curtis is next with 29 FA cup games.

• Richard Shaw's total is up to the end of season 2004-05.

ARM WRESTLING
Three Coventry City players never to be messed with on the pitch, were equally tough in the "sport" of arm wrestling.

Centre-half Roy Barry can lay some claim to be "Muscle Man." When the Sky Blues toured the Far East in 1972, they visited South Korea. Enter Mr. Kim, manager of the restaurant at the Munwha Hotel, whose proud boast was that he was unbeaten in three

Roy Barry

years of arm wrestling. Scotsman Barry couldn't resist the challenge and bets were placed.

In a best-of-three contest, Roy won the first "Battle of Biceps" but his team-mates thought Mr. Kim might be holding back. It was not the case.

In a teeth-gritting, vein-bulging display, Roy Barry won the next two bouts hands down. The City players were rewarded with free drinks for the night and the next day Mr. Kim had his arm in a sling.

"That Mr. Barry," said the defeated champ, "sure is a strong fellah. He would make a wonderful wrestler."

The captain of the 1987 FA Cup winning team, Brian Kilcline, is also quite handy at arm wrestling. In January 2002, a Sky Soccer television programme had a challenge entitled "Nifty Fifty." The contestants were footballers competing for a prize of £50 per win. "Killer" Kilcline took on and beat the biceps of Robbie Savage, Lee Clark of Fulham and Derby's Darryl Powell. The only men to leave Kilcline limp-wristed were Neil "Razor" Ruddock and a man later to become a Sky Blue, Dele Adebola.

TOP 30 APPEARANCES FOR COVENTRY CITY

1. Steve Ogrizovic	601	(1984-00)
2. George Curtis	538	(1955-69)
3. Mick Coop	492	(1966-81)
4. Brian Borrows	477	(1985-97)
5. Bill Glazier	395	(1964-75)
6. Mick Kearns	382	(1957-68)
7. Tommy Hutchison	355	(1972-80)
8. George Mason	350	(1932-52)
9. Roy Kirk	345	(1952-60)
10. Richard Shaw	335	(1995-)
11. Trevor Peake	325	(1983-91)
12. Ron Farmer	315	(1958-67)
13. Frank Austin	313	(1953-63)
14. Peter Hill	303	(1949-62)
15. Willie Carr	292	(1967-75)
16. Ernie Machin	288	(1962-72)

Brian Borrows (above) and Mick Coop

17. Michael Gynn	286	(1983-93)
18. Brian Hill	284	(1958-71)
19. Cyrille Regis	279	(1984-91)
20. Noel Simpson	270	(1948-57)
21. Dick Mason	263	(1946-55)
22. Ronnie Rees	262	(1962-68)
23. Dave Clements	257	(1964-71)
24. Lloyd McGrath	253	(1982-94)
25. Brian Roberts	249	(1976-84)
26. Alf Wood	246	(1937-51 & 1956-58)
27.=Martin McDonnell	245	(1949-55)
27.=Billy Lake	245	(1928-39)
29. Clarrie Bourton	241	(1931-37)
30.=Chris Cattlin	237	(1968-76)
30.=Jimmy Dougall	237	(1920-26)

INCLUDED: League, FA Cup, League Cup, Charity Shield, Europe and substitute appearances.
NOT INCLUDED: Appearances in optional cups (e.g. Southern Professional Floodlit Cup, Texaco, Full Members, Simod, ZDS). Also not included: testimonials, friendlies and tour matches.

Note: The appearance totals for George Curtis and Mick Kearns. have been adjusted down from those which appeared in *Sky Blue Heaven Vol I*. They no longer include five appearances by Curtis in the Southern Professional Floodlit Cup or Kearns' three appearances in the same competition.

ARENA

Coventry City's new stadium, the Ricoh Arena, opened on August 20, 2005 for a league game against QPR. Safety officials restricted the attendance to 23,043. Few projects in the city had a more difficult birth but when the day came, the wait was worth it.

The £113m project, which includes a concert hall, a banqueting suite, a hotel, a health and fitness suite, a proposed casino and, of course, a football stadium, is one of the most ambitious projects ever developed in the Midlands.

City's new home holds 32,000 spectators around a pitch that measures 105 metres by 68 metres. The builders reported that a staggering 35,000 cubic metres of rubble was moved out and 5,500 tonnes of material brought in. A total of 4,000 tonnes of grass seed was used on the pitch.

The Ricoh Arena gives the Sky Blues a fantastic stage. All that is needed now is a team to do it justice.

ATKINSON, RON

One of the biggest names and hat sizes in football came to Highfield Road in February 1995 when "Big Ron" arrived as manager. The former boss of West Bromwich Albion, Manchester United and Sheffield Wednesday joined Coventry City shortly after leaving Aston Villa. He replaced Phil Neal who had been sacked.

Excitement over the appointment added 5,000 to the crowd for Atkinson's first match in charge, on Februray 18. City beat West Ham United 2-0 with an impressive debut by Ron's first signing for the club, former England International Kevin Richardson. City were undefeated in Ron's first six games and the Sky Blues climbed to ninth in the Premiership. Atkinson was voted Manager of the

Ron Atkinson

Month for his first month in charge. The most impressive performance was a 3-2 win at Liverpool as Peter Ndlovu scored a hat-trick. The future looked rosy.

City's cheque book came out as champagne and players were purchased with equal relish. The new players over the coming weeks included David Burrows, goalkeeper John Filan and most significantly, Gordon Strachan as player-assistant manager. Then inexplicably the form deserted the side and in the next six games, City lost five and won just once. They diced with a relegation spot, but avoided it with a stunning 3-1 win at Tottenham as Ndlovu, Strachan and Julian Darby all, as Ron would say, "played blinders". At the end of the season, Coventry finished 16th in the table.

During the summer of 1995 Big Ron spent almost as much time in transfer activity as he did working on his sun tan. It looked good on paper, even if some of the signings were a little over-priced. New men Paul Williams from Derby County (£1m), John Salako from Crystal Palace (£1.5m) and

Paul Telfer from Luton Town (£1.15m) all made their debuts in the opening game of the 1995-96 season, a 3-0 defeat at Newcastle United. The results did not pick up. In the first 16 games of the season, the Sky Blues won once and by December, were bottom of the table.

A steady stream of players flowed in during the season, including Richard Shaw from Crystal Palace (£1m), Noel Whelan from Leeds United (£2m), Eoin Jess from Aberdeen (£1.75m) and Liam Daish from Birmingham City (£1.5m). However, the team clearly never equalled the sum of its parts and some of the players hardly registered. Brazilian Isaias from Benfica (£500,000), a Portuguese unknown Carlita (£250,000), and Nii Lamptey from Aston Villa (£150,000) soon disappeared. Isaias was destined not to feature in the side following a bust-up with Gordon Strachan.

City became big-spending under-achievers as Big Ron's outlay reached £13m before the end of the season. The club finished in 16th place again and avoided the drop place on goal difference. By any reckoning it was a very poor outcome for the money invested.

In the close season of 1996, Coventry City swooped to make the biggest signing in the club's history to that date. The £3m transfer of Gary McAllister from Leeds United showed the club had ambition, but again things did not dramatically improve. Moreover, Atkinson was not fully involved in this particular move. The chairman and Strachan had done the deal. Behind the scenes, Strachan was preparing for the arranged hand-over in July 1997 when Atkinson would step down.

However, when Ron proposed to sign Carlton Palmer, Strachan voiced reservations. He wanted a veto on players who he thought would become

his own responsibility or problem in the coming season. Atkinson and Strachan, the two old friends were no longer singing from the same hymn sheet. (Ironically, Strachan did sign Palmer in due course, in September 1999 and his brief but successful spell with the Sky Blues justified Atkinson's opinion.)

By the end of October 1996, City had won once in 12 league games and were yet again in the drop zone. In a night of the long knives, after a draw at Everton, Ron moved upstairs to become Director of Football, with Strachan taking over as team manager. Atkinson was furious that the arrangement was leaked to the press by a board member; from then on he was surplus to requirements.

By the summer of 1997, with the role as Director of Football unclear and unwanted, he left the club. He had splashed the cash in his 20 months at City but the results had not improved. There wasn't even a cup run for the fans to get excited about. Flamboyant Big Ron had lost his touch.

Manager: February 1995 – October 1996. Director of Football: October 1996 – June 1997.
Managerial Stats: P74 W19 D28 L27 25.6% wins

ATTENDANCES
The highest attendance for any Coventry City match remains the FA Cup Final in May 1987 when 98,000 people packed into Wembley. Even if the Sky Blues reach the Final again, this figure will not be surpassed as the new Wembley stadium holds only 90,000 spectators.

The second highest attendance for any Coventry City match was in 1937 when 68,029 saw City take on Aston Villa at Villa Park. That figure was almost exceeded in 2001 when 67,637, including a massive turnout from the Sky Blue Army who filled their allocation, saw Coventry City take the lead at Old Trafford against Manchester United and hold the champions at 2-2 until nine minutes to go. This attendance was all the more remarkable as the game was a 12 noon kick-off and was being televised live.

City's highest home attendance looks like it will never be beaten. The legendary 'Midlands Match of the Century' against Wolverhampton Wanderers in April 1967 – which effectively decided the destination of the Second Division title – had 51,455 crammed into Highfield Road, with many of them sitting on the grass around the perimeter of the pitch and climbing the floodlights.

As the new Ricoh Arena has a 32,000 capacity, this match will remain the record for the foreseeable future.

At the other end of the spectrum, it is interesting to note that the three lowest home league attendances came in the 1920s when, not surprisingly, City were at a sorry ebb. The lowest of the low was against Hartlepools United (as it was called then).What a miserable day it must have been on Saturday April 24 1926 when only 1660 hardy loyalists turned up to see this Third Division (North) fixture. But they were the wise ones, as City won 5-2.

Low turnouts to meaningful matches have been rare in recent times but one that did stand out was the FA Cup Third Round tie against Crewe in January 2005. Only 7,629 turned up – making this the lowest home attendance for a proper FA Cup tie (that is, excluding qualifying rounds) in City's long history.

For a full record of High and Low Attendances, see Appendix.

AUSTIN, FRANK

An accomplished and reliable performer, Austin was a loyal servant to the club in more than 300 games and over a period of some ten years. Sadly, he was with Coventry City during a turbulent period and he never got the chance to display his talents at the top level.

A former England schoolboy international, Austin was signed by manager Harry Storer from Nottinghamshire side Toton in 1950. He made his City debut on April 11, 1953 against Newport County, a 1-0 home defeat. Frank played as a wing half for three seasons before a switch to left back position in 1956. He continued to be an automatic choice for the side. In the 1959-60 season he missed just five out of the 48 games played.

It was quite an achievement to be a regular selection in the team. During his City career Austin played under eight managers as Coventry struggled along in Divisions Three South, Three and Four of the football league.

Frank was not part of manager Jimmy Hill's long term plans and he left for Torquay United in the middle of the "Big Freeze" of January 1963. He played just 24 games for the Devon side before moving to Southern League Chelmsford City in July 1964. One of the longest serving players in the history of Coventry City, Frank Austin passed away in July 2004.
1953-63. 313 apps. 2 goals.

AUTHOR ! AUTHOR!

Coventry City managers or players who have at some time written a book. (Not listed – those who have been the subject of a book.)

Atkinson, Ron *A Different Ball Game.* Andre Deutsch 1998
Barratt, Harry *Crown Green Bowls Rules of the Game.* Crowood Press 1988.

Butcher, Terry *Butcher: My Autobiography.* With Bob Harris. Highdown, 2005
Cantwell, Noel *United We Stand.* Stanley Paul 1965
Hateley, Mark *Home and Away.* With Tony Francis. Stanley Paul 1986
Hateley, Mark *Top Mark!* With Ken Gallacher Mainstream 1993
Hill, Jimmy *Striking for Soccer.* Peter Davis 1961
Hill, Jimmy *Improve Your Soccer.* Penguin, 1966
Hill, Jimmy *Golden Goals.* With Brian Moore Cleveland Petroleum 1972
Hill, Jimmy *Football Crazy.* Robson 1985.
Hill, Jimmy *The Jimmy Hill Story: My Autobiography* Hodder & Stoughton 1998 Coronet (paperback) 1999
Mercer, Joe *The Great Ones.* Oldbourne 1964
McAllister, Gary *Captains Log.* With Graham Clark Mainstream 1995
Neal, Phil *Attack from the Back.* Arthur Barker, 1981
Neal, Phil *Life at the Kop.* With David Vear Macdonald, 1986
Pearce, Stuart *Psycho.* Headline, 2000
Quinn, Mick *Who Ate All The Pies?* With Oliver Harvey Virgin, 2003
Raynor, George *Football Ambassador at Large.* Stanley Paul 1960.
Reid, Peter *Everton Winter, Mexican Summer.* Macdonald 1997
Roberts, Brian *Harry's Game: A Sideways Look at Football.* Paper Plane 1991
St. John, Ian *The Saint: My Autobiography.* Hodder & Stoughton 2005
Strachan, Gordon *An Autobiography.* With Jack Webster Stanley Paul 1984
Strachan, Gordon *Strachan Style: A Life in Football* With Ken Gallacher Mainstream 1991
Yorath, Terry *Hard Man, Hard Knocks* With Grahame Lloyd Celluloid 2004

AWAY COLOURS

(continued from Sky Blue Heaven Vol I)
2002-03 Yellow Shirts and Shorts/ 3rd. kit-Dark Blue Shirts and Shorts
2003-04 White Shirt with Wide Red Band/Red Shorts

2004-05 "Ajax" Kit. White Shirt with Wide Red Band, Red Shorts
2005-06 Black Shirts, Black shorts

BADGES

To write a history of Coventry City enamel badges – produced by supporters and by the club – would be a massive undertaking. So instead here's a completely subjective overview of some of the oddest, and most outstanding examples of the genre.

Badges, like most things are a product of their time. One of the most interesting is this one which is most likely from the early 1970s.

With its sharp pointed fins at the top it looks more like an oriental weapon to be thrown at a deadly foe.

It also has a curious thistle-like motif at the top – perhaps a tribute to the many great Scots City had at the time. Instead of the conventional hard enamel, it is protected by a coating of plastic – an innovation that was never likely to catch on.

If that was an unusual shape then stranger was to come with this double circle effort which incorporated City's tramline kit, introduced in 1977, and a bizarre SUPPORT THE BEST bubble above it. One for the true believer.

Music and football periodically collide and this Two Tone Coventry City badge is the most recent

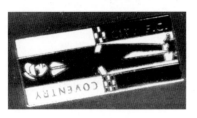

example. Issued in the early 1980s, it linked Coventry City FC with the Rude Boy emblem of the Two Tone label (and used by Coventry bands The Specials, The Selecter, and others).

The fact that the badge was oblong was also unusual, but perhaps the most shocking shape of any badge came with this official badge in the mid-1990s which superimposed the Coventry City crest on an outline associated with Manchester United. The Red Devils' badge is uniquely shaped and the fact that Coventry City

"borrowed" it was either cheeky or blatant, depending on your point of view.

Into the 21st century, Sky Blues fanzines continued to be active on the badge front, none more so than Twist 'n' Shout, whose prolific production of Sky Blue Army pin-ons included this simple but effective sky blue elephant-and-ball device while the badge from the Gary Mabbutt's Knee fanzine incorporated the

City battle-cry PLAY UP SKY BLUES.

But one fan badge went back further. In 2002 the Coventry City Supporters Club produced a replica of a badge which pre-dated the Sky Blue era when City were the Bantams It was a badge which confused a younger generation of City fans and sometimes was even worn by Sky Blues supporters to disorientate their Tottenham Hotspur-supporting mates who would often mistake it for a Spurs cockerel.

BARRATT, HARRY
The son of Southampton player Joe Barratt, Harry was a long serving player and a significant figure in the history of the club.

Harry Barratt was born on December 25 1919 in Headington, Oxford. He played for Coventry boys and then Alfred Herbert's factory side before signing for City in 1934. He went out on loan to non-league Cheltenham Town before making his debut for Coventry against Blackburn Rovers in April 1938. During the war he scored 44 goals for City's wartime side in over a hundred appearances and also made guest appearances for Leicester.

He was ever present in the 1945-46 interim season in the Football League South, which is statistically excluded from records.

Barratt's career at Coventry got going post-war as he became a fixture in the team and captained the side. Although he was a wing half, versatile is the best way to summarise Harry Barratt. He played in every position for City except left-back during his career, and even played in goal during a game when keeper Alf Wood was injured.

He was forced to retire through a knee injury after one game of the 1951-52 season. After retiring from playing at the age of 32, Barratt became manager of Rugby Town. He kept his links with Highfield Road. In November 1954 Coventry signed Bill Patrick from Snowdown Colliery Welfare in Kent, following Harry's recommendation.

In the summer of 1955, City installed a new management set-up under Jesse Carver, with Harry Barratt appointed chief scout. He soon got down to business and recommended another young player from Snowdown Colliery, named George Curtis.

Two further players arrived at Highfield Road from Snowdown as Barratt recommendations – Alf Bentley and Eric Jones.

Harry Barratt left City in September 1956, "relieved of his duties" in a torrid time behind the scenes at the club. He continued scouting for the club on a part time basis while working as manager of Snowdown Colliery FC.

In July 1958 he was appointed manager of Gillingham and was boss of the Kent side for four years until 1962.

Barratt took up the sport of bowls and went on to become National Coach for the British Crown Green Bowls Association.

In 1988 he wrote a book on the rules of the sport.

Harry Barratt died in Coventry in 1989.
1938-51. 176 apps. 12 goals.

BEST, JERRY
Jerry Best holds the record for being City's shortest ever goalkeeper at just 5'7" (1.70m.) tall.

Born on April 22, 1897, Jerry Best played for his home town Mickley Colliery Welfare in Northumberland before joining Coventry City in May 1920.

Best was goalkeeper for City in Coventry's difficult early days in League Football. He took over from Joe Mitchell mid-way through the 1920-21 season in Division Two, and he made his debut on December 25th 1920 against Cardiff City in a 2-4 defeat.

Agile and safe between the posts, Best went on to become the first player to make 200 appearances for the club. He was ever-present for three seasons in succession, between 1922-23 and 1924-25.

His achievement is remarkable given that Best had suffered an injury to his arm while serving in the Army in World War One.

It was a disappointment to the fans when Coventry sold Best to Halifax Town in 1926. The move came about when the players were asked to take a cut in wages. Best refused the new deal and was on his way.

He played just nine games for Halifax before moving to Rotherham where he played 26 matches before moving into non-league football at both Newark and Worksop.
1920-26. 236 apps.

BIRMINGHAM CITY CONNECTIONS

There have been many players on the move along the A45 from Sky Blues to Blues and vice versa. Listed below are the direct transfers only between the two clubs.

To Birmingham:

Fred Hawley	(1919-20. 14 apps.)
Jackie Randle	(1922-27. 156 apps.)
Jackie Brown	(1936-38. 73 apps. 29 goals)
Bill Bradbury	(1950-54. 24 apps. 7 goals)
Tommy Briggs	(1950-51. 11 apps. 7 goals)
Eddy Brown	(1952-54. 89 apps. 51 goals)
Tony Hateley	(1968-69. 20 apps. 5 goals)
Jim Blyth	(1972-82. 174 apps.)
Brian Roberts	(1976-84. 249 apps. 2 goals)
Jim Hagan	(1978-79 & 1980-82. 19 apps.)
Gerry Daly	(1980-84. 101 apps. 22 goals)
Nicky Platnauer	(1983- 84. 53 apps. 7 goals)
Greg Downs	(1985-90. 177 apps. 7 goals)
David Smith	(1988-93. 177 apps. 19 goals)
Kevin Drinkell	(1989-92. 52 apps. 7 goals) *loan*
Peter Ndlovu	(1991-97. 196 apps. 41 goals)
David Burrows	(1995-00. 130 apps.)

From Birmingham:

Frank Crowe	(1919-20. 2 apps.)
Joe Godfrey	(1919. 6 apps.)
Archie Smith	(1919. 1 app.)
Billy Walker	(1919-20. 22 apps. 8 goals)
Bert Millard	(1920-22. 68 apps. 9 goals)
William Morgan	(1920-22. 57 apps. 14 goals)
Wallace Clark	(1924-25. 7 apps.)
Bernard Smith	(1936-40. 57 apps.)
Fred Gardner	(1945-49. 13 apps. 3 goals)
Don Dearson	(1947-50. 88 apps. 11 goals)
Alex McIntosh	(1948-49. 20 apps. 3 goals)
Martin McDonnell	(1949-55. 245 apps.)
Don Dorman	(1951-54. 94 apps. 31 goals)
Ken Rowley	(1954-55. 3 apps.)
Mick Ferguson	(1984. 7 apps. 3 goals) *loan*
David Rennie	(1993- 96. 92 apps. 3 goals)
John Gayle	(1993-94. 6 apps.)
Chris Whyte	(1995. 1 app.) *loan*
Liam Daish	(1996- 97. 34 apps. 3 goals)
Gary Breen	(1997-2002. 171 apps. 2 goals)

Martin Grainger	(2004. 7 apps.) *on loan*
Stern John	(2004-
Ian Bennett	(2005. 6 apps.) *loan*

Coventry City stats in brackets.

BLACK, ERIC

Scotsman Eric Black played for the successful Aberdeen team of the 1980s. They were Scottish Champions and Cup winners, winning the European Cup Winners Cup in 1983.

In 1988 he left to play in the French League for Metz. When an injury cut short his playing career, he stayed on in France to do his coaching badges under Aimé Jaquet and Gérard Houllier.

At the same time, he did some scouting for Metz. He was in France five years before returning to Scotland. Black managed Motherwell and then served as assistant manager at Celtic in the 1998-00 season.

When Gary McAllister appointed Black as his assistant in the summer of 2002, it was not the case of an old mate helping another out – the two had not worked together previously. It was just that McAllister had heard good things about his fellow-Scot and considered Black the best man for the job.

Eric Black

Following the resignation of McAllister, Black was appointed Coventry City manager on January 15 2004, having already been caretaker-manager for several weeks.

Black was given an 18 month contract, until the end of the 2004-05 season and started his reign as City manager like no other before him, with a 6-1 away win at Walsall on January 17, 2004. It couldn't carry on like that, although with home wins of 4-0 and 4-1 against Burnley and Preston North End in March, the Sky Blues were playing entertaining football.

They were inching up the table, but good wins were undone by losses. A top six finish and the play-offs became out of reach. Nevertheless, it looked as if Black was making progress and the sides he put out were capable of scoring goals.

So it was a major shock to most Sky Blues fans when Black was sacked on May 1st. 2004, following a 5-2 win at Gillingham. He had been given three and a half months in charge. Along with Black, first team coach Archie Knox and goalkeeping coach Alan Hodgkinson were also shown the door.

Eddy Brown (right) in full flight, in a Birmingham City game against Aston Villa. The Villa player (left) is Jimmy Dugdale, uncle of Alan Dugdale, a Coventry City man in the 1970s.

Fans staged protests at Black's sacking, but he was gone and replaced by Peter Reid with one game of the season remaining. In July 2004 Eric Black was appointed first team coach at Premier League Birmingham City.

Assistant Manager: June 2002 – January 2004.
Manager: January 2004 – May 2004.
Managerial Stats: P26 W12 D4 L10 46.1% wins

BROWN, EDDY

Centre-forward Eddy Brown was born in Preston on February 28, 1928 and played for North End before moving to Southampton in 1950 and was top scorer two years running at the Dell.

Two years later he was bought by Coventry City manager Harry Storer deep into the 1952-53 season for a £7,000 fee. Storer hoped that Brown's goalscoring prowess would keep City in Division Two. Brown managed three goals in nine games but it couldn't save City from being relegated to Division Three(S).

However, over the next two seasons the fans were

treated to a goalscoring blitz by Brown. With lightning pace and anticipation, Eddy Brown formed a deadly partnership with Don Dorman. In the 1952-53 season he scored 19 goals in 31 appearances. City finished sixth in Division Three(S).

The next season Brown did it again, hitting 20 goals in 34 appearances.

Eddy was nothing if not theatrical. He was an early exponent of celebrating goals in an unusual way, shaking hands with the corner flag after he scored. Not only that, but in press conferences he was in the habit of quoting passages from Shakespeare.

The 1954-55 season began well with eight goals in 12 games for the Bantams before he was sold to Birmingham City for £10,000.

It was a classic sale for non-footballing reasons, a short term balancing the books act. Brown and Birmingham were the winners. They reached the FA Cup final in 1956 and qualified for Europe in the early days of the Fairs Cup.

Brown continued his impressive scoring ratio at St Andrew's playing 185 games for the Blues, scoring 90 goals. After retiring Eddy Brown returned to Preston and became a school teacher. 1952-54. 89 apps. 51 goals.

BUTCHER, TERRY

When Coventry City chairman John Poynton sacked John Sillett in November 1990 he was replacing one of the most experienced coaches in the game and the only man to bring a major trophy to the club with a player-manager of no previous managerial experience. It was a gamble on a massive scale.

Not that centre-half Terry Butcher was anything

other than a distinguished and respected player as captain of Ipswich Town, Rangers and England. He had played in three World Cup tournaments and won 77 caps.

But a mid-season shake-up was not what Coventry needed and Poynton's desire for a big-name manager would backfire and cost both himself and the club dearly.

Butcher's appointment didn't improve matters even for a honeymoon period. The Sky Blues went six league games under his stewardship before claiming their first win, a 2-0 defeat of Tottenham Hotspur on December 26, 1990.

As the season wore on, Butcher made some changes, with Tony Dobson and Steve Livingstone leaving for Blackburn Rovers and David Speedie for Liverpool, with Ray Woods from Wigan Athletic, former England team-mate Kenny Sansom from Newcastle United, Stewart Robson on loan from West Ham and Robert Rosario from Norwich City (£650,000) all arriving.

The team's form picked up and the switch of Kevin Gallacher to a striking role paid dividends, as he hit the target 16 times.

As a player for Coventry City, Butcher appeared in City's colours just seven times before becoming injured. His role as a steadying influence in the heart of the defence was destined to be unfulfilled. As the signing of Butcher had required a £400,000 fee to Rangers, it was a costly as well as a strategic gamble to sign him.

During the summer of 1991, Terry Butcher signed the outstanding Robson full-time and added striker Paul Furlong from QPR and Peter Ndlovu from Bulawayo Highlanders in Zimbabwe. Ndlovu had first been brought to the club's attention on a

Terry Butcher

summer tour when John Sillett gave him a trial and Butcher too saw the potential.

However, Butcher was his own man in other ways, showing no sympathy to the FA Cup heroes Cyrille Regis and Brian Kilcline who both left. Before the season even started he had also had a fall out with two more Cup winners.

Lloyd McGrath and Trevor Peake along with Kenny Sansom broke a curfew during a pre-season tour of Scotland by having a beer in Troon less than 48 hours before a friendly with Ayr United.

Butcher threw the book at them, fining the players and placing all three on the transfer list. It came over as a heavy-handed excuse to dish out the message that "I'm boss around here."

Initially, the season 1991-92 showed an improvement in position, if not form. Inconsistent

Coventry reached fifth in the table in October, but it was a false dawn.

Off-the-pitch matters continued to divert the fans' and players' attention. Everyone at the club seemed determined to fall out with each other, and a boardroom shake-up would resonate to the training camp.

With Peter Robins replacing John Poynton as chairman, "cost-cutting measures" were implemented by the new board and Butcher's assistant manager Mick Mills along with reserve team manager Brian Eastick, were sacked.

Whether this represented a real saving is debatable as City were already involved in a compensation dispute with coach Dixie McNeil who was sacked following Butcher's appointment. Mills and Eastick would also cost the club dearly for the early termination of their contracts and furthermore, the experienced Don Howe, brought in as coach, was presumably not working for peanuts. Not for the last time, a club would demonstrate that a fool and his money soon go separate ways.

Butcher did make an attempt at a comeback on the pitch in a Zenith Data Systems match against Aston Villa in October 1991 but he was sent off and announced his retirement from playing.

As winter closed in, the team slipped down the league and were knocked out of the League Cup by Tottenham. Terry was negotiating signing a defender from Moor Green, David Busst, but it would be his successor Bobby Gould who eventually gave the player his debut.

The new chairman saw a team in decline and after a home defeat in the league to Spurs (again) along with a miserable draw at home to Cambridge in the

FA Cup, he showed Butcher the door. Robins further justified the sacking by criticising Butcher for taking an enlarged salary as a player-manager when he didn't play and was manager only.

In the end it a court case, which was heard some time later, to finally close this unhappy chapter. The verdict came down in favour of Butcher who was awarded a six-figure compensation settlement.

Butcher moved to Sunderland in 1992 and miraculously resurrected his playing career becoming player-manager in 1993, succeeding Malcolm Crosby. More recently he managed Motherwell as well as working as a pundit on radio and television.

1990- 91. 7 apps. Player-Manager: November 1990 – January 1992.
Managerial Stats: P60 W20 D14 L26 33.3% wins.

CARETAKER MANAGERS

Charlie Elliott	1954-55	*33 games*
Bob Dennison	1972	*12 games*
Don Mackay*	1984-85	*7 games*
George Curtis/John Sillett*	1985-86	*3 games*
Don Howe	1992	*20 games*
Phil Neal*	1993	*4 games*
Roland Nilsson*	2001	*13 games*
Steve Ogrizovic/Trevor Peake	2002	*1 game*
Steve Ogrizovic/Trevor Peake	2004	*1 game*
Adrian Heath	2005	*3 games*

* Position made full-time.
League and cup games included.

CONSECUTIVE GAMES, SCORED IN
Don Dorman scored hat-tricks in consecutive home games, against Crystal Palace on November 29 1952 and against Torquay United on December 13 1952.

SCORING IN CONSECUTIVE GAMES

10 Clarrie Bourton	19 goals	10 league games	Sept. to Nov. 1931. Division 3(S).
9 Clarrie Bourton	13 goals	9 league games	Jan. to Mar. 1933. Division 3(S).
8 Ray Straw	11 goals	7 league & 1 cup game	Nov. to Dec. 1958. Division 4.
7 Jimmy Loughlin	11 goals	4 league & 3 cup games	Nov. to Dec. 1929. Division 3(S).
7 Terry Bly	9 goals	7 league games	Nov. to Dec. 1962. Division 3.
6 Mick Quinn	9 goals	6 league games	Nov. to Dec. 1992. Premier League.
6 Les Jones	9 goals	5 league & 1 cup game	Dec. to Jan. 1934-35. Division 3(S).
6 Clarrie Bourton	8 goals	6 league games	Sep. 1935. Division 3(S).
6 Bobby Gould	6 goals	6 league games	Mar. to Apr. 1967. Division 1.
6 Ted Roberts	6 goals	6 league games	Oct. to Nov. 1950. Division 2.
5 Arthur Bacon	14 goals	5 league games	Dec. to Jan. 1933-34. Division 3(S).
5 Tom Crawley	9 goals	5 league games	Dec. to Feb. 1939. Division 2.
5 William Paterson	7 goals	5 league games	Nov. to Dec. 1925. Division 3(N).
5 Bryn Allen	7 goals	5 league games	Apr. to May 1950. Division 2.
5 Billy Lake	7 goals	4 league & 1 cup game	Nov. to Dec. 1930. Division 3(S).
5 Jock Lauderdale	6 goals	5 league games	Mar. to Apr. 1932. Division 3(S).
5 Clarrie Bourton	6 goals	5 league games	Apr. 1933. Division 3(S).
5 Dave Clements	5 goals	5 league games	Mar. to Apr. 1965. Division 2.
5 Andy Morrell	5 goals	5 league games	Sep. to Oct. 2003. Division 1.

City won the Division 3(S) games, 4-2 and 7-2 respectively. Dorman also scored an away goal in between those two in an FA Cup game at Bishop Auckland (W 4-1) and two more in the next league match at Swindon Town (W 3-2). His total was an impressive nine goals in four consecutive games.

The king of the Coventry City consecutive scorers though was Clarrie Bourton who managed 19 goals in ten consecutive games in 1931 and 13 in nine consecutive games 18 months later.

In the modern era, Micky Quinn, the man City supporters nicknamed 'Sumo' for his rotund figure, stands out as the only player to score in five consecutive games or more in the top flight for Coventry. Quinn scored in six matches in succession in 1992, bagging an incredible nine goals in his run.

More recently, Andy Morrell managed five in five in 2003.

CRICKETERS

The days when football clubs allowed all-rounders to play professional football in the winter and cricket in the summer may have passed, but City's history is illuminated with such remarkable sportsmen.

One of the most outstanding was **Don Bennett**, who was born in Wakefield on December 18, 1933, but having moved south with his family at the age of seven, played cricket for Middlesex not his native Yorkshire.

He was a right-hand middle-order batsman and right-arm medium bowler. Bennett scored 10,656 runs in county cricket and took 784 wickets, scoring 1000 runs in a season twice. His top score was 117 not out and he hit four centuries. In a distinguished county career which spanned from

1950 to 1968, Bennett appeared 392 times for Middlesex.

As a footballer, Bennett joined Coventry City from Arsenal where he had failed to make the first team. With City, Bennett played at full-back between 1959-62 (77 apps.) and was captain under the management of Billy Frith.

In August 1961, Bennett was allowed to miss the first three games of the football season while completing the cricket season for Middlesex. It's hard to imagine that happening nowadays.

He left Coventry in the close season of 1962 to join Hereford United. Bennett subsequently returned to the summer game and was cricket coach for Middlesex for many years.

He was responsible for the Middlesex first XI up to his retirement in 1997. He is now Chairman of the Cricket Committee and a life vice-president of the county.

Charlie Elliott had a long and distinguished career at both cricket and football. Elliott was born in Bolsover in 1912 and was signed for Coventry by Harry Storer from Chesterfield in July 1931, having previously been on the books of Sheffield Wednesday.

He was a Coventry City player either side of World War Two, 1931-48 (101 apps. 2 goals). During the war he played in more than 150 games for City as well as both Nottingham clubs.

At Highfield Road he played mostly as defensive cover in the full-back position when first choice players were injured. He made 12 appearances in the 1935-36 Division Three(S) Championship season. In the first full season after the war, he made 29 appearances, his most consistent run in the side, but he decided to retire from playing in the close season of 1948. By his own admission Elliott was an average footballer, but nothing else about the man was average.

As a cricketer, Charlie first appeared for Derbyshire in 1932. He was an opening batsman for the county and played in the same cricket side as Storer.

The two were in the 1936 County Championship winning side – the same year that City won the Third Division (South) title, thus achieving the remarkable feat of winning a Championship in two sports in one year.

Elliott's highest score was a double century with 215 against Notts at Trent Bridge in 1947. He hit 1000 runs in a season six times and appeared in 275 matches for Derbyshire scoring a career total 11,965 runs. He was also an off-break bowler and an outstanding slip fielder. He put away his pads for the last time in 1953.

Elliott rejoined Coventry City the same year as chief scout and, following the resignation of Jack Fairbrother, took over as caretaker-manager of Coventry between November 1954 and April 1955.

After the appointment of Jesse Carver as manager, Charlie reverted to the scouting role. As a scout for City he discovered Lol Harvey, Frank Austin, Bill Bradley and Ray Sambrook. He resigned in October 1955 to rejoin his old mentor Harry Storer at Derby County for a short spell as assistant manager at the Baseball Ground.

Calling time on his football career, Elliott returned to cricket becoming a County umpire in 1956 and a Test umpire the following year. He stood in no less than 42 Test matches and five One Day Internationals.

His last Test as an umpire was England v. Pakistan at Lords in 1974. He spent six years as an England cricket team selector and was awarded an MBE for his services to cricket. For a further ten years he was chairman of Derbyshire's cricket committee and was elected Life President of the club in 1994. Charlie obviously didn't know the meaning of the word retirement and he ran a guest house in West Bridgford, near the Trent Bridge cricket ground, until shortly before his death on New Years Day 2004, aged 91.

Born in Coventry on June 4, 1922, **Freddie Gardner** was principally a cricketer who also played football. An opening batsman, Gardner made his first appearance for Warwickshire in 1947 and went on to hit 17,905 runs in his career. His highest score was 215 not out against Somerset at Taunton in 1950. In total he hit 29 centuries including 110 against the Australians. He hit 1000 runs in a season ten times.

As a footballer, Gardner was on Birmingham City's books before the war, during which he made guest appearances for Northampton and Port Vale. He signed for Coventry City in 1945 and made his debut in September 1946 against Newcastle United in a 1-1 draw.

An inside forward, Gardner played 13 games between 1946-49, scoring three goals. He moved on for a short spell at Newport County, then returned to play part-time for Rugby Town and Leamington.

Gardner continued his cricket career with Warwickshire completing 338 matches by the time he finished playing in 1961. Fred umpired for two years and coached young cricketers in the Coventry area up to his premature death in January 1979 at the age of 56.

Patsy Hendren was regarded by cricket writer and broadcaster John Arlott as the best batsman he had ever seen. Only one cricketer in the whole history of the game – Sir Jack Hobbs – hit more centuries than Hendren.

What makes Patsy Hendren's achievements even more remarkable is that his cricket career only took off as his football career was coming to an end.

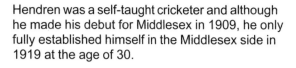

Born in Chiswick in 1889, Elias Henry O'Hanrahan was known as Patsy because of his Irish ancestry. Hendren was quite a character and known for his wit and mimicry. As a footballer, he played for QPR, Brentford and Manchester City before moving to Highfield Road.

He scored twice on his Coventry City debut in October 1909 at Watford in a 3-0 win.

In total he made 33 appearances for City as an inside forward, scoring 14 goals between 1909-11 in the Southern League. After suffering a knee injury his appearances were limited and he re-joined Brentford from Coventry in 1911.

Hendren served in World War One with the Sportsman's Battalion. After the war, he played in one of the 1919 Victory International football matches. Several "Home Internationals" were staged around the British Isles and Hendren played for England against Wales at Ninian Park. Wales won 2-1.

He continued playing for Brentford in the post war years and by the time he hung up his football boots, he had been on their books for a total of 17 years.

Hendren was a self-taught cricketer and although he made his debut for Middlesex in 1909, he only fully established himself in the Middlesex side in 1919 at the age of 30.

A middle order batsman and slow bowler, Hendren made his Test debut in the 1920-21 tour of Australia in the First Test in Sydney. He went on to play in 51 tests for England, hitting seven centuries. He scored 3,525 runs for England and is the eighth oldest England cricketer, having played in a Test Match at the age of 46.

His greatest triumph was a score of 205 not out against the West Indies at Port of Spain, Trinidad in 1929, one of four double-centuries during the tour. In his three tours of Australia he averaged 60 runs per innings.

In 1933 Hendren caused a sensation by batting against the West Indies' fast bowlers in a special cap made by his wife. It had three peaks, two of which covered his ears and temples. The cap was lined with sponge rubber and must be considered a forerunner of the modern helmet, years ahead of its time.

Patsy scored a remarkable 57,611 first class runs in his career, for England and Middlesex. This included 170 centuries, making an average of 50.8 runs per innings. He collected 725 catches along the way. His older brother Denis also played for Middlesex and was an umpire.

After retiring from playing cricket in 1938, Hendren became a cricket coach at Harrow School and then coached for four years at a school in Sussex. He became a life member of the MCC in 1949 and was also on the Middlesex committee. An England International in two sports, Patsy Hendren died in London in 1962, aged 73.

As a footballer, **Arthur Jepson** was a goalkeeper for Port Vale, Stoke City and Lincoln City, but he didn't play for Coventry City. His role at Highfield Road was chief scout in Billy Frith's second spell as manager in the late 1950s. When new manager Jimmy Hill brought in his own backroom staff, Jepson was sacked in November 1961.

A cricketer for Nottinghamshire, Jepson was a hard-hitting lower order batsman and right arm fast-medium bowler. He was a late starter, playing his first county match at the age of 23, but he went on to play 390 matches for Notts between 1938-59, scoring 6,369 runs. Jepson took 100 wickets in a season once and took 1,051 career wickets. His best bowling was 8 for 45 against Leicestershire at Trent Bridge in 1958.

In 1960 he became a first class umpire and stood in four Test Matches and five One Day Internationals. In 1971 he umpired the Gillette Cup Final between Lancashire and Gloucestershire, which has become famous as the "Lamplight Match." With a 30,000 crowd at Old Trafford, play did not finish until 8-50pm. The winning captain of Lancs, Jack Bond, asked umpire Jepson afterwards if he had ever heard of bad light. "What's that up there?" replied Jepson. "The moon," Bond said. "Well how far do you want to see?" said Jepson. Arthur Jepson died in 1997 aged 82.

An amateur cricketer, **Jack Lee** appears in this section by virtue of just one first class appearance for Leicestershire in 1947. In that game he took a wicket with the first ball he bowled.

Obviously a man who was keen on first impressions, Lee also managed to score a goal on his debut for Coventry City in 1954. Jack Lee was with City for just one season 1954-55, making 18 appearances and scoring ten goals. His

distinguished football career prior to joining Coventry had included one England cap while with Derby County and an FA Cup runners-up medal in 1950.

John Mitten – the son of Charlie Mitten, who famously played for Newcastle United and Manchester United – turned out for Mansfield Town, Newcastle United and Leicester City before joining Coventry in July 1963.

He was a squad player in the Sky Blue era, filling in mostly at outside left. He made 41 appearances in a four year period before transferring to Plymouth Argyle in January 1967. He later played for Exeter City, Bath City and Tiverton Town. In the summer game, Mitten was wicket keeper with Leicestershire between 1961-1963, playing 14 matches and taking 23 catches. As a batsman he played 23 innings and made a top score of 50 not out.

The former Coventry City chairman **Bryan Richardson** played 40 matches for Warwickshire between 1963-67. He was an opening left hand batsman and leg break bowler. He scored a total of 1,323 runs for the county, with a highest score of 126. Both his brothers were also cricketers – Derek for Worcestershire and Peter for both Worcestershire and Kent.

As well as being a successful businessman and chairman of Coventry City, **Derrick Robins** was also a keen cricketer. He appeared in two county matches for Warwickshire in 1947, playing as a lower order right-hand batsman and wicket-keeper. Robins also played minor counties cricket for Warwickshire as wicket-keeper, between 1946-52. He became a member of the Warwickshire club committee and was instrumental in creating the knock-out cup for county cricket which began in 1969.

Steve Ogrizovic in action for Coventry & North Warwicks CC. See Cricket Shorts

Robins played his final first class match for his own XI in 1971 against The West Indies. The Derrick Robins XI was a regular feature on the cricket calendar for many years. A great patron of cricket, he took teams on regular overseas tours including each winter from 1972-73 to 1979-80. When the Derrick Robins XI toured South Africa in the winter of 1972-73, it marked the first time that a South African Invitation XI had assembled for three years. (see: Robins, Derrick).

Born in Liverpool on February 2, 1898, **Harry Storer** played county cricket for Derbyshire. His father, Harry senior, also played for Derbyshire and football for both Arsenal and Liverpool.
Harry Storer was an opening right hand batsman and leg-break bowler. He scored 13,513 runs and took 232 wickets for Derbyshire.

Coincidentally, 232 was also the number for his highest score as a batsman v. Essex at Derby in

1933. He hit 1000 runs in a season six times. He was also an occasional wicket keeper. Storer managed to close his account as a cricketer with the County Championship in 1936. It was a special year for him as his Coventry team had secured the Division Three(S) Championship in May.

Unusually, Storer combined playing cricket with football management. Following his appointment as Coventry City manager in 1931, Harry continued his cricket career with Derbyshire during the summers. In all, he appeared in 302 matches between 1920-36.

Harry Storer was a major figure in the history of Coventry City. He was manager twice between 1931-45 and 1948-53 for a total of 19 years. (see: Storer, Harry. Sky Blue Heaven Vol. I).

Robert Turner was the first county cricketer to play for Coventry City. Known as "Leggy," he was a middle-order right hand batsman and a bowler. Between 1909-11 he played in 20 matches for Leicestershire, scoring 525 runs and taking nine wickets. His father had also played for Leicestershire.

Football was Turner's main game and he had a good career with Leicester Fosse, Everton, Preston North End and Darlington before joining Coventry in 1914.

City were then a Southern League side and with the advent of World War One, Turner's appearances were limited to just 14. An outside left, he scored his only goal in a 10-1 thrashing of Newport in November 1914. He joined the Army in 1915 and survived the Great War to live to the age of 74. He died in Darlington in 1959.

Born in Chilvers Green, Nuneaton in 1911 and known as "Ken," **Kilburn Wilmot** was a lower order right-handed batsman and right arm fast paced bowler. Wilmot played for Warwickshire from 1931-39. In 75 matches he took 154 wickets and he played 101 innings, scoring 871 runs.

For Coventry City, Wilmot made 12 appearances in the 1932-33 season in Division Three(S). Left-back was his position and he made his debut in a stunning 7-0 victory over QPR in March 1933.

He wasn't needed for the next season and he moved on to play for Nuneaton, Walsall and Dudley before finishing with football in 1936. He died in 1996 in his home town of Nuneaton.

CRICKET SHORTS

Steve Ogrizovic played Minor Counties cricket for Shropshire 1983 and 1984. A fast bowler, not as might be expected a wicket-keeper, he played in cup games against Warwickshire and Yorkshire, including the match when Shropshire knocked Yorkshire out of the Nat West Cup. In a non-competitive match, also in 1984, he bowled out Viv Richards, one of the game's greatest ever batsman. Unfortunately, it was a no-ball and Richards proceeded to knock the next ball out of the ground. Oggy also played regularly for Coventry & North Warwickshire in the Birmingham League.

***

In July 1987, the FA Cup winning team played a charity cricket match against Coventry & North Warwickshire. The match at Binley Road was in aid of the West Midlands Centre for the Disabled.

***

Coventry City Manager **Noel Cantwell** played cricket for Ireland in 1956. A left hand batsman and right arm bowler, he appeared in the International match between Scotland and Ireland in Edinburgh, June 1956. According to the football writer Brian Glanville, Essex representatives once watched Cantwell making 47 runs against New Zealand and asked him to join that county. Cantwell turned this down saying that he "didn't want to spend his whole year in England!"

***

Coventry City put out a cricket team on occasions in the late 1930s in charity matches and during the 1960s Sky Blue era, City fielded a six-a-side cricket team in charity or testimonial matches, and in the annual Wellesbourne six-a-side tournament. **George Curtis, Mick Kearns, Brian Hill and Bobby Gould** were among those who played.

***

Former England and Kent wicket-keeper **Godfrey Evans** was the first compere of Radio Sky Blue at Highfield Road during the 1963-64 season.

***

Don Nardiello

Good amateur cricketers and Coventry City footballers: **Harry Boileau, Ernie Machin, Don Nardiello; Ray Gooding; Steve Ogrizovic; Carl Lightbourne.** Nardiello, in spite of his Italian parentage, was a good cricketer and had the choice between a career as a footballer or a county cricketer.

***

Andy Goram, goalkeeper (City player 2001. 7 apps.) played cricket for Scotland. A wicket-keeper, he has three cricket caps, including one for a match against Australia.

***

Jim Cumbes the Worcestershire cricketer and ex-goalie for West Bromwich Albion, Aston Villa and Tranmere Rovers, was on Coventry City's books briefly in 1976. As goalkeeping cover in case of injuries, he played six reserve games for the Sky Blues. Cumbes was a right arm seam bowler and took 379 wickets in a 19-year first class career. He is currently chief executive of Lancashire CCC.

***

Jim Meunier (City player 1914-15. 11 apps.) was league professional with New Brighton C.C.

CROSS, DAVID

David Cross was no stranger to a suitcase, a road map and a hotel guide in his playing career, with more than ten clubs to his name. However, it's a credit to him that fans of any of the clubs he played for, claim him as one of their own favourites.

Born in Bury, David Cross joined Rochdale from school. An old-fashioned centre-forward in the best sense, always in the thick of the action, he was particularly good in the air. When Coventry were knocked out of the FA Cup by Rochdale in January 1971, one of the Rochdale goalscorers was Cross, with a header.

He moved on to Norwich City the same year, before joining Coventry City in November 1973 for

David Cross (centre) with Brian Alderson (left) and Mick Coop (right)

a £150,000 fee. Cross always wanted to be first to the ball and was fearless in the penalty area. At the time he joined the Sky Blues, he had broken his nose five times in the previous four years.

Manager Gordon Milne put him into the line-up alongside striker Colin Stein. The partnership was only occasionally successful and Cross also played alongside Alan Green, Brian Alderson, Donal Murphy and Mick Ferguson in an effort to find the right mix. Cross's best season at Highfield Road was 1975-76 when he hit a total of 16 goals and was top scorer. He hit six of those in hat-tricks on the opening and closing games of the season.

Don't be fooled, though; that was as good as it got and Coventry finished 14th.

His personal favourite goal for Coventry was a diving header against Sheffield United in March 1975 in a 2-2 draw.

Cross was a bit of a character. One story relates to room sharing at away games. Whenever he shared a hotel room with a first team debutant, just before switching off the light, he would tell the younger man that he couldn't sleep without a goodnight kiss, which at home his wife always gave him. Sure enough the room-mate was persuaded to tip-toe to Cross' bed and give him a peck on the cheek. The next day nothing was said, but team-mates teased the youngster, puckering up their lips and so on.

With Mick Ferguson fulfilling his potential as the leading striker, Coventry accepted a bid of £200,000 from West Bromwich Albion for Cross in November 1976. Just over a year later he was on the move to West Ham United, where he would enjoy his most successful period.

He also played against Coventry in a dramatic League Cup Semi-Final, which the Hammers won. (see: League Cup) The remaining clubs that David Cross played for were: Manchester City, Vancouver Whitecaps, Oldham Athletic, Vancouver Whitecaps (again), West Bromwich Albion (again), Bolton Wanderers, Bury, Blackpool and lastly a side in Cyprus. He retired from playing in 1987, having played 553 games, scoring 194 goals.

After retirement, David Cross sold insurance and coached youth players at Bolton before joining the coaching staff at Oldham Athletic.

He worked there in several capacities, working his way up to the position of assistant manager to Iain

Dowie. He was among several men to lose their jobs in cost cutting measures in February 2003. 1973-76. 106 apps. 36 goals.

CUP DISASTERS
In order for there to be Sky Blue Heaven, there has to be Sky Blue Hell. Cup disasters fall into two categories. There are those clubs who always seem to knock City out (the Repeat Offenders) and those real horrors (the One-Off Giant Killings). Look away now if you don't wish to be reminded of the scores.
(Home team listed first).

THE REPEAT OFFENDERS
Burnley

Burnley 5, Coventry City 0 FA Cup R1	1910-11
Burnley 2, Coventry City 0 FA Cup R4	1946-47
Burnley 2, Coventry City 0 FA Cup R4	1951-52
Coventry City 0, Burnley 1 League Cup R2	1971-72
Coventry City 1, Burnley 2 League Cup R2	1982-83

Rochdale

Rochdale 2, Coventry City 1 FA Cup 6 QR	1920-21*
Rochdale 2, Coventry City 1 FA Cup R3	1970-71
Rochdale 2, Coventry City 0 FA Cup R4	2002-03

(Rochdale also beat City 1-0 in a League Cup tie in 1991, but on this occasion the Sky Blues went through on aggregate, having won the first leg 4-0.)

Tranmere Rovers

Tranmere 3 Coventry City 2 FA Cup PR R	1923-24
Tranmere 2 Coventry City 0 FA Cup R4 R	1967-68
Tranmere 5 Coventry City 1 League Cup R2	1999-00

THE ONE-OFF GIANT-KILLINGS

Coventry City 0 Luton Town 1 FA Cup R1 R	1919-20*
Southport 1 Coventry City 0 FA Cup 6QR	1921-22*
New Brighton 3 Coventry City 0 FA Cup 5QR	1922-23*
Worksop T 1 Coventry City 0 FA Cup R1	1925-26*
Scunthorpe 4 Coventry City 2 FA Cup R1 R	1935-36*
Workington 3 Coventry City 0 League Cup R1	1961-62
Coventry City 1 Kings Lynn 2 FA Cup R2	1961-62*
Sutton United 2, Coventry City 1 FA Cup R3	1988-89*
Northampton T 1, Coventry City 0 FA Cup R3	1989-90

Scarborough 3 Coventry City 0 League Cup R2   1992-93

Coventry City 0, Gillingham 1 League Cup R3 R 1996-97

Colchester U 3 Coventry City 1 FA Cup R4 R   2003-04

*Non-League Opposition. R = Replay

PR = Preliminary Round

QR = Qualifying Round

Never mind! Confucius says, *"To be victim of giant-killing, first you have to be a giant."*

CUP FINALS – NEARLY STAGED

Two major Cup Finals might have been played at Coventry City's Highfield Road ground.

FA Cup Final, 2nd Replay – Chelsea v Leeds United, April 1970. The match would have been at Highfield Road, but the outcome was decided at Old Trafford in the first replay. Chelsea won 2-1, after the teams had drawn 2-2 at Wembley.

League Cup Final, Replay – Aston Villa v Tottenham Hotspur, March 1971. This game would have been on March 10th if the match at Wembley was drawn after extra-time. Highfield Road was not required as Spurs won the final 2-0. Ex-Coventry skipper George Curtis was in the Villa squad, but missed the chance to play in a Cup Final at Highfield Road.

DEBUTANTS

At the start of the 1926-27 season, no less than ten of the team that ran out to face Northampton Town were making their debuts for Coventry City. Defender Charles Houldey was the only man to keep his place in the side.

Michael Gynn

Manager James Kerr's clearout was not an immediate success, however, as the side full of strangers lost 3-0 at home.

In the modern era, the start of season 1983-84 saw five players – Ashley Grimes, Michael Gynn, Terry Gibson, Dave Bamber and substitute Nicky Platnauer – make their debut on the opening day. Away at Watford, City won 3-2. In their next match of the season, three more players – Trevor Peake, Micky Adams and substitute Graham Withey (who scored) – made their debuts against Spurs. The teams drew 1-1 at White Hart Lane.

A year later, four men made their debuts on the opening day of the 1984-85 season – Steve Ogrizovic, Brian Kilcline, Martin Jol and Kirk Stephens. Facing Aston Villa away, the new look Sky Blues lost 1-0.

Another year on, in 1985-86, full backs Brian Borrows and Greg Downs made their debuts together on the same day at the start of the season.

The highest number making their debut in modern times was in the opening match of 2003-04 season. On August 13, 2003 in a home League Cup first round tie against Peterborough United, no less than eight players made their first appearance in a competitive game for Coventry.

The players appearing for the first time were: Scott Shearer, Stephen Warnock, Micky Doyle, Patrick Suffo, Graham Barrett, Claus Jorgensen, Dele Adebola and substitute Andy Morrell. City won 2-0, with debutants Barrett and Adebola the goalscorers.

Three days later, in the first league game of the season, eight players made their league debuts for the club. There was one change from the Cup game, with Steve Staunton making his debut, while Jorgensen was an unused substitute.

DEFEATS

WORST DEFEATS, HOME

1-8 v Leicester City League Cup R5 Dec 1 1964
1-6 v Liverpool Division 1 May 5 1990
0-5 v Tottenham Division 2 Aug 30 1919
0-5 v Everton Division 1 Sep 27 1980
1-5 v Notts County Division 1 Feb 16 1982
1-5 v Newcastle Utd Premiership Sep 19 1998
2-5 v Southend Utd   Division 3 Mar 13 1964
0-4 v Leeds Utd Division 2 Feb 4 1950
0-4 v Tottenham Premiership Dec 31 1994
0-4 v Manchester Utd Premiership Nov 22 1995
0-4 v Portsmouth Division 1 Mar 19 2003
1-4 v Fulham FA Cup R1 Nov 24 1928
1-4 v Plymouth Argyle Division 3(S) Apr 13 1929
1-4 v Hull City Division 2 Sep 8 1951
1-4 v Millwall Division 3(S) Nov 23 1957
1-4 v Arsenal Division 1 Mar 31 1984
1-4 v Liverpool Division 1 Aug 29 1987
1-4 v Manchester Utd Division 1 Oct 21 1989
1-4 v Sheffield Wed Division 1 Mar 17 1990
1-4 v Crystal Palace Premiership Nov 2 1994

WORST DEFEATS, AWAY

2-10 v Norwich City Division 3(S) Mar 15 1930.
1-9 v Millwall Division 3(S) Nov. 19, 1927.
1-8 v Doncaster Rovers Division 3(N) Jan 23 1926
1-8 v Exeter City Division 3(S) Dec 4 1926
2-8 v Southampton Division 1 Apr 28 1984
0-7 v Walsall Division 3(S) Feb 11 1928
1-7 v Swansea Town Division 2 Aug 30 1951
1-7 v Southampton Division 3(S) Feb. 22 1958
1-7 v West Brom Division 1 Oct. 21 1978
0-6 v Everton Division 1 Nov. 26 1977
1-6 v Cardiff City Division 3(S) Sep 14 1931
1-6 v Watford Division 3 Sep 11 1962
1-6 v. West Brom League Cup R4 R Nov 10 1965
1-6 v West Brom Division 1 Oct. 9 1968
1-6 v Arsenal Division 1 May 11 1991
1-6 v. Chelsea Premier League Oct 21 2000

DOUGALL, JIMMY

Scotsman Jimmy Dougall gave good service to the club in the early days of league football at Coventry City. He was the second player in the club's history after Jerry Best to make more than 200 appearances for the team. Dougall was born in 1900 in Wishaw, North Lanarkshire, and played for Cleland Juniors and the Scottish junior team.

He was recommended to the Coventry manager Harry Pollitt and came south to join City at the age of 19. Dougall made his debut against Luton Town in an FA Cup tie in January 1920. An outside right, he made an immediate impression and soon found himself a regular in the side.
His tricky wing play supplied plenty of crosses for the forwards. Although Dougall didn't score many goals, City at the time struggled to hit the net from any source.

Over seven seasons of struggle in Division Two, Dougall was one of City's few players of quality. He came to the attention of bigger clubs, but Coventry turned down lucrative offers for him.

Following an outstanding display against Manchester United at Old Trafford, when he scored a goal in a 2-1 win, City received a £2,000 bid from United, but it was turned down.

At the end of the 1925-26 season, the players were asked to take a cut in wages. Dougall declined the reduced terms and moved on to Reading for a nominal fee. He suffered a broken leg after only 12 games and his career was brought to a premature close.

As with many Coventry City players over the years, Dougall felt most at home in the city of Lady Godiva and returned to the area to work at Morris

Engines.
1920-26. 237 apps. 14 goals.

EARTHQUAKE

The Sky Blues may have made the earth move, according to one expert.

The construction of the Ricoh Arena required the demolition of a Foleshill Gasometers and the event took place on the morning of Saturday, September 21, 2002.

This, according to at least one geological specialist, may have been a contributing factor in the country's biggest-ever earthquake.

The Gas Towers

Geotechnical consultant Alan Cook says that this probably had a "knock-on effect" on surrounding rocks. The tremor's epicentre was in Dudley, only 25 miles away.

While the British Geological Survey say it was "highly unlikely" the incidents were related, Mr. Cook says the gasometer demolition may have been a contributing factor to the main cause – the build-up of pressure in tectonic plates.

He said: "It was a big explosion, a big crash of material hit the ground. It has to have had an effect on the local stress on the local rocks and that just may have had the knock-on effect of releasing the stress elsewhere."

But Glenn Ford, a senior seismologist at the BGS, threw cold water on the idea. "Large demolitions are going on all the time, such as blocks of flats or at quarries.

"The amount of energy involved is insignificant compared with an earthquake." Mr. Ford obviously did not share the same feeling for drama as his film star namesake.

ENGLAND INTERNATIONALS
See Sky Blue Heaven Vol I

ENGLAND INTERNATIONALS (WITH OTHER CLUBS)
The following Coventry City players, managers or coaches won full England Caps either before or after their stay with City, but not during:

Jesse Pennington 25 caps *1907-20* Player 1918-19
Danny Shea 2 caps *1914* Player 1923-25
Fred Morris 2 caps *1920* Player 1924-25
Billy Kirton 1 cap Player 1928-30
Austen Campbell 8 caps *1923-29* Player 1919-20
John Ball 1 cap *1927* Player 1930-31
Harry Storer 2 caps *1924-28* Manager
1931-45 & 1948-53

Dick Hill 1 cap *Millwall 1926* Trainer 1935-49
Wilf Copping 20 caps *1933-39* Coach 1956-60
Joe Mercer 5 caps *1938-39* Manager/
director 1972-81
Jackie Lee 1 cap *1951* Player 1954-55
Alan Hodgkinson 5 caps *1957-61* Goalkeeping
coach 2002-04
Don Howe 23 caps *1958-60* Manager 1992
Ray Pointer 3 caps *1962* Player 1965-67
Gordon Milne 14 caps *1963-65* Manager 1972-81
Terry Paine 19 caps *1963-66* Youth coach 1988-90
Tony Waiters 5 caps *1964-65* Coach 1971-72
Larry Lloyd 4 caps *1971-80* Player 1974-76
Jeff Blockley 1 cap *1973* Player 1969-72
Mick Mills 42 caps *1973-82* Coach 1990-92
Gerry Francis 12 caps *1975-76* Player 1981-83
Phil Neal 50 caps *1976-84* Manager 1993-95
Bob Latchford 12 caps *1978-79* Player 1984-85
Peter Barnes 22 caps *1978-82* Player 1984-85
Kenny Sansom 86 caps *1979-88* Player 1990-93
Terry Butcher 77 caps *1980-90* Player-manager
1990-92
Nick Pickering 1 cap *1983* Player 1986-88
Steve Hunt 2 caps *1984* Player 1978-84
Mark Hateley 32 caps *1984-92* Player 1978-83
Peter Reid 13 caps *1985-88* Manager 2004-05
Stuart Pearce 78 caps *1987-00* Player 1983-85
Mick Harford 2 caps *1988-89* Player 1993
John Salako 5 caps *1991-92* Player 1995-98
Carlton Palmer 18 caps *1992-94* Player 1999-01
Tim Flowers 11 caps *1993-98* Player 2002
Kevin Richardson 1 cap *1994* Player 1995-98
Tim Sherwood 3 caps *1999* Player 2004-05

Players are listed chronologically according to the date of their first England appearance.

FEWEST LEAGUE DEFEATS
6   1966-67 Division 2 *Champions*
8   1963-64 Division 3 *Champions*
9   1933-34 Division 3(S)

9   1935-36 Division 3(S) *Champions*
9   1965-66 Division 2

FEWEST LEAGUE GOALS CONCEDED
38   1970-71 Division 1
42   1988-89 Division 1
43   1966-67 Division 2 *Champions*
44   1991-92 Division 1
44   1997-98 Premier League

FEWEST LEAGUE GOALS SCORED
35   1919-20 Division 2
35   1991-92 Division 1
37   1970-71 Division 1
38   1996-97 Premier League
39   1989-90 Division 1

FEWEST PLAYERS USED
19   1929-30 Division 3(S)
20   1968-69 Division 1
20   1975-76 Division 1
20   1982-83 Division 1

FEWEST POINTS SCORED
(2 Points For A Win)
29   1919-20 Division 2
31   1924-25 Division 2 *relegated*
31   1927-28 Division 3(S)
31   1968-69 Division 1
33   1967-68 Division 1
33   1971-72 Division 1

FEWEST POINTS SCORED
(3 Points For A Win)
34   2000-01 Premier League *relegated*
38   1995-96 Premier League
41   1996-97 Premier League
42   1998-99 Premier League
43   1985-86 Division 1

FEWEST LEAGUE WINS
8   1995-96 Premier League
8   2000-01 Premier League *relegated*
9   1919-20 Division 2
9   1967-68 Division 1

9   1971-72 Division 1
9   1996-97 Premier League

FREAK GOALS

We kick-off in 1927 when Coventry scored a goal that was not allowed. In an away game against Aberdare, City won a corner. The ball hit referee in the stomach causing him to blow his whistle by mistake and then it went into the goal. The referee disallowed his "own goal" but it didn't matter too much, as Coventry went on to win the match 7-0.

***

Roy Kirk scored from 80 yards against Northampton Town in an FA Cup first round match November 29, 1954. Former Coventry goalie Alf Wood, too far off his line, couldn't reach Kirk's clearance. It was the winning goal in the game. Kirk, naturally enough, claimed he intended to score although, as he was on the edge of his own penalty area at the time, it seems unlikely.

***

In May 1963 Coventry conceded a goal that wasn't, against Shrewsbury Town. John Gregson's shot went into the goal through the side netting, but the referee awarded a goal. It proved to be the winner as City lost the game at Gay Meadow, 2-1.

***

Clive Allen of Crystal Palace thought he had scored in a Division One game against City in September 1980. The ball struck the stanchion at the back of the net and rebounded at speed back onto the pitch. Amazingly, the referee waved play on and the Sky Blues went on to win 3-1. The incident was seen on television and resulted in the re-design of goal net supports.

***

On January 4, 1975, in an FA Cup third round tie against Norwich City, Larry Lloyd cleared the ball from inside his own half. The ball flew 50 yards into the net without bouncing past the Canaries goalie Keelan. The first half strike gave Coventry a 2-0 lead and passage into round four.

***

Steve Ogrizovic's famous goal against Sheffield Wednesday on October 25 1986 is thought to be the last time a keeper has scored from his own area. *See Sky Blue Heaven Vol I, Goalkeepers.*

***

Steve Ogrizovic

Dion Dublin scored an unusual goal against Newcastle United on November 8, 1997. A City attack was foiled leaving Dublin off the pitch beyond the goal line.

The Magpies' goalie Shay Given failed to notice the Sky Blues striker behind him. As he rolled the ball out in front of him prior to a clearance, Dublin came alongside and nonchalantly stroked the ball into the open goal. Newcastle protested to no avail and City won 2-1, with Dublin adding a second.

FRIENDLIES

Coventry City has a long history of playing friendly games. What is surprising is how many of those matches have been played during the season, both home and away.

The "Big Freeze" of the 1962-63 winter saw City travel three times to Ireland where the pitches were not frozen. Manager Jimmy Hill took City to Dublin, Cork and Belfast in February 1963. In the first game, against Manchester United, 15,000 turned up and Third Division City acquitted themselves well against Matt Busby's mighty Red Devils in a 2-2 draw.

For the next two games in Ireland, Coventry shared the plane over with their opponents Wolves. They got some match practice but lost both times, by scorelines of 0-3 and 3-6.

To celebrate winning the Division Three Championship in 1964, City embarked on an incredible sequence of five matches in five days. Just two days after beating Colchester United to seal the promotion, the Sky Blues flew to Dublin to play a Dublin XI at Dalymount Park, home of Bohemians. The Monday match was won by the home side 4-3.

There was no time for a refreshing glass of stout as the next night they were back at Highfield Road to face Tottenham Hotspur. A party atmosphere was guaranteed with an entertaining 6-5 win for Spurs. On the Wednesday, April 29th, City travelled to neighbouring Bedworth United and won at a stroll 4-0. City had just enough time to clean their kit before the next run out.

They returned from Bedworth to play America. Not *in* America but *against* America. Even the go-ahead Sky Blues couldn't get across the Atlantic so fast. This was America FC, a touring Brazilian side. George Hudson scored twice but the superior visitors won the game 5-2.

If it's Friday, it must be – Eastbourne. Not the most obvious opponents but this was also a charity benefit match. The Sussex side went down 3-1 to a Coventry team that included manager Jimmy Hill in the side. It is believed to be only time that he played for City.

This fifth match of the sequence was also City's sixth in seven days, including the last league game. They took a three-week rest before another away friendly was played in Spain against Onteniente.

A curious friendly was played later the same year, 1964. A two-legged fixture named the "Enterprise Cup" was played against Scottish side Greenock Morton. The Cup was originated when newspapers nominated Morton and Coventry as the most enterprising clubs in British football.

In October 1964, a crowd of 17,000 saw the sides draw 2-2. Bill Glazier, City's new goalkeeper, made his debut.

It was March of the following year before the return leg took place. The game was played in a snowstorm, and the Scots, no doubt more accustomed to such playing conditions, ran out winners 5-3 on aggregate.

City's biggest win in a friendly was in October 1966 when they beat Ashford Town 11-0. Quite why they travelled to Kent in midweek to play a minor league side is a bit of a mystery, but the shooting practice set City up for a Championship winning run in Division Two that season.

City have twice won friendly home games by an 8-0 scoreline. In a pre-season friendly in 1976, the victims were the now-defunct Coventry Sporting. Eight different names got on the scoresheet: Alan Green, Donal Murphy, John Beck, David Cross, John Craven, Jimmy Holmes (pen), Garry Thompson and an own goal.

Amazingly, the other team on the end of an 8-0 thrashing by the Sky Blues were German side Kaiserslautern.

The floodlit game at Highfield Road in November 1963 came in the middle of a stunning run of form for Jimmy Hill's Division Three side. City were undefeated in seven league and cup games in which they had scored 25 goals. George Hudson's hat-trick was the middle one of three consecutive hat-tricks. The victory spurred City on to the Division Three Championship.

The autumn has been a traditional time for the club to play friendly games. In October 1965 Coventry arranged a friendly at Highfield Road against F.C. Biel from Switzerland. The match, however, was cancelled.

The Swiss team, despite coming from the hometown of Rolex, Omega and Swatch, displayed poor timekeeping by pulling out at the last minute. Coventry officials were angry at the short notice they were given and reported the matter to FIFA. It is not known if the Swiss-based world body took any action.

City, determined to play a game, asked Manchester City to fulfil the fixture and Joe Mercer's side obliged, losing 4-2 into the bargain.

It was only a week since the clubs had met in the League Cup when Coventry had won 3-2.

Coventry City's link up with American 'soccer' led to a friendly at home in 1981. The visitors were Washington Diplomats in whom City had invested heavily. Ex-Southampton men Trevor Hebberd and Malcolm Waldron were in the Diplomats side, but they were given some capital punishment in a 5-1 defeat. The Sky Blues scorers were Garry Thompson (3), Tommy English and Mick Coop.

Despite the result, an American style shoot-out was staged after the game. Five players from each side were given five seconds to score, starting from 35 yards out. The Americans won the shoot-out 3-2. City scorers were Peter Bodak and Andy Blair. Blair scored with a penalty, awarded when he was brought down during his run. It was thus an unusual penalty within a shoot-out. The men who missed were Gary Bannister, Gary Gillespie and Danny Thomas.

Apart from friendly games with other clubs, Coventry have also played against national sides on occasions. At Highfield Road the club has defeated Japan, Zimbabwe and Pakistan each time by a 2-0 scoreline. In August 1978, goals from Terry Yorath and Mick Ferguson saw off Japan.

In a pre-season friendly in 1983 with Zimbabwe Graham Withey and guest player Charlie George got the goals. The same scoreline was the outcome of a game against Pakistan in 2001. David Thompson and John Aloisi scored this time. On overseas tours, the Sky Blues have faced the Faroe Islands, Finland, Saudi Arabia, South Korea, Thailand, Tunisia and Zimbabwe.
See also Overseas Games, Pre-Season Competitions, Summer Tours and Testimonials Away.

Kevin Gallacher

GALLACHER, KEVIN

A club record fee of £900,000 brought Kevin Gallacher from Dundee United to Coventry City in January 1990. City manager John Sillett had tracked the player for some time. Gallacher came from a football family; his father William and Grandfather Patsy both played for Celtic.

Around the same time that City won the FA Cup in 1987, Gallacher had played in the UEFA Cup Final for Dundee United. The Scottish side were beaten 2-1 on aggregate by IFK Gothenburg (who,

incidentally, had Roland Nilsson in their side).

In 1988 he won his first Scotland cap. Despite these high profile advertisements of his talents, Coventry were the sole English team willing to gamble on him.

Although Gallacher inspired a surge up the table in the 1989-90 season that saw Coventry reach fourth place in Division One in March, it was a short-lived honeymoon.

That season Gallacher scored three goals in 17 matches and City finished just below mid-table. Playing Gallacher as a winger was clearly not working.

The following season, 1990-91 didn't begin much better for Gallacher. By November when manager John Sillett was sacked, Gallacher had scored just one league goal in a 3-1 win against Everton in the first home game of the season.

A thrilling League Cup fourth round tie against Nottingham Forest got the goals flowing. City won 5-4 and Gallacher hit a hat-trick.

After the departure of David Speedie in January 1991, manager Terry Butcher switched Gallacher to a central striking role. By the season's close Kevin was top scorer with 16 goals. Sky Blues fans had a new favourite and voted him Player of the Year.

The achievement was all the greater as he had missed seven games after a knee operation. He had an all-round game for a striker. Fast and comfortable with the ball at his feet, Gallacher was good in the air and a deadly finisher.

The next season, Gallacher scored twice in a 5-0 win over Luton Town including an overhead kick goal. But dark clouds were on the horizon and another change of manager came in January 1992 when Butcher was sacked and replaced by Don Howe.

Howe's negative tactics saw both the team and Gallacher go six games without a goal. In March he suffered a hamstring injury against Nottingham Forest. Although he returned for the last three games of the season, he couldn't add to his tally of ten goals for the season.

Gallacher returned to the Scotland squad gaining ten caps as a Sky Blue. In 1992 he played in the European Championships in Sweden. In total in his international career, he would win 53 caps.

The 1992-93 season began well with Bobby Gould returning as manager. In October 1992 a Sunday newspaper claimed that Gallacher was about to move to Celtic for £2m. but the rumour had no foundation. Gallacher's season was blighted by injuries unfortunately and he was in and out of the side. A hamstring injury kept him out for a month in the autumn. When he was fit, he was in the thick of the action but he only managed to score six times in 23 games.

By March 1993, speculation was rife that Gallacher would be sold in a need to raise cash. Nine clubs were reported to be interested in signing him, but he didn't move to any one of those. Instead, Kenny Dalglish of Blackburn Rovers came in just before the transfer deadline.

A part-exchange deal was done, with Roy Wegerle moving in the opposite direction. Gallacher's valuation in the deal was £1.5m., with the USA International Wegerle rated at £500,000.

Gallacher had made a good career move, winning a Championship Medal in 1995. He scored against the Sky Blues in a 4-0 hammering at Ewood Park in January 1997, but suffered injuries which robbed him of the best part of two seasons at Blackburn. After six years at Blackburn Rovers, Gallacher moved to Newcastle United in October 1999.

He was Bobby Robson's first signing after becoming manager. Injuries continued to blight him and in August 2001 he moved to Preston North End before playing briefly at Sheffield Wednesday and Huddersfield Town over the next year or so.

1990-93. 117 apps. 35 goals.

GOALKEEPERS

Coventry City fielded three different goalies in three consecutive games and kept three clean

Jim Blyth

sheets in August and September 1979. Jim Blyth, Steve Murcott and Les Sealey were the safe hands and the achievement was unique at the time.

***

Scott Howie, on loan from Motherwell, made only one appearance for City in a friendly against Bayern Munich on January 27, 1998. *(See: Friendlies at Highfield Road, Mid Season)* He flew from Glasgow to Birmingham airport to begin his loan period, and on arriving at Ryton, found he was playing that same evening.

Howie was a non-playing substitute for two FA Cup

ties and one league game, but did not make an appearance in full competition for City.

Curiously, the same keeper also holds the rare distinction of playing in two games in one day. On February 16, 1993, he played for Scotland U-21 against Malta at Tannadice, Dundee (k.o. 1-30pm. Result 3-0) That night Howie played for Clyde against Queen of the South (Division Two. Result 2-1).

**

Unfortunate is the only way to describe Alan Miller's stay at City. He made just one substitute appearance and conceded six goals. Miller came on to replace Chris Kirkland, sent off in a Premier League game in October 2000 at Stamford Bridge against Chelsea.

The experienced former Middlesbrough and WBA stopper had arrived on loan from Blackburn Rovers only 24 hours earlier.

His first task was to pick a penalty out of his net. Miller was not blamed for the heavy defeat and after a month during which he was an unused substitute, he returned to Ewood Park. Kirkland's sending off was subsequently nullified on appeal.

**

During season 2001-02, Coventry used five different goalkeepers. Three goalies played in three consecutive games in the autumn. Magnus Hedman, Andy Goram and Gary Montgomery played against Barnsley, Gillingham and Chelsea (League Cup) on September 25, 29 and October 9. None kept a clean sheet.

**

In the autumn of 2003, City went one better and used three goalies in two games. At Sunderland on November 8th. they started with Pegguy Arphexad between the posts, but he was injured and was replaced by Scott Shearer at half time. For the next match, at home to Gillingham, Gavin Ward was chosen to make his debut in goal.

GOALIES 1997-2005

Magnus Hedman	1997-02	151 apps.
Chris Kirkland	1999-2001	29 apps
Alan Miller	2000	1 app *sub on loan*
Andy Goram	2001	7 apps
Gary Montgomery	2001-03	9 apps
Tim Flowers	2002	5 apps *on loan*
Morten Hyldgaard	2002-03	31 apps
Fabien Debec	2002-03	13 apps
Scott Shearer	2003-05	41 apps
Pegguy Arphexad	2003-04	5 apps
Gavin Ward	2003-04	12 apps
Luke Steele	2004-05	36 apps *on loan*
Ian Bennett	2005	6 apps *on loan*

Up to the end of the 2004-05 season. For a full list of City goalkeepers 1964-2001, see Sky Blue Heaven Vol I

GOALSCORING RECORD HOLDERS

Coventry City have a history of signing players with a scoring pedigree. The following players were the season's top scorers of league goals in all divisions prior to arriving at Highfield Road:

Terry Bly	1960-61	52 goals
Peterborough United. Division Four		
Mick Quinn	1989-90	32 goals
Newcastle United. Division Two		
Lee Hughes	1998-99	31 goals
West Bromwich Albion. Division One		
Shaun Goater	2001-02	28 goals
Manchester City. Division One		
Andy Morrell	2002-03	34 goals
Wrexham. Division Three		

● Terry Bly scored seven hat-tricks towards his total and two more goals that season in the FA Cup. With Coventry City he had one season, scoring 28 goals in 42 appearances.

GOALSCORERS
COVENTRY CITY'S TOP TWENTY OF ALL TIME

1.	Clarrie Bourton	182	(1931-37)		11	Cyrille Regis	62	(1984-91)
2.	Billy Lake	123	(1928-39)		12	Ian Wallace	60	(1976-80)
3.	Ted Roberts	86	(1937-52)		13	George Lowrie	59	(1939-48 & 1951-53)
4.	Frank Herbert	86	(1922-29)		14	Mick Ferguson	58	(1974-81 & 1984)
5.	Ray Straw	85	(1957-61)		15	Ronnie Farmer	53	(1958-67)
6.	Peter Hill	78	(1949-62)		16	Ronnie Rees	52	(1962-68)
7.	George Hudson	75	(1963-66)		17	Terry Gibson	51	(1983-86)
8.	Leslie Jones	73	(1934-38)		18	Eddy Brown	51	(1952-54)
9.	Dion Dublin	72	(1994-98)		19	Ernie Hunt	50	(1968-73)
10.	Jock Lauderdale	63	(1931-37)		20	Garry Thompson	49	(1977-83)

Terry Gibson

INCLUDED: League, FA Cup, League Cup and Fairs Cup.
NOT INCLUDED: Goals scored in optional cups. e.g. Texaco, Full Members, Simod, ZDS. Also not included – testimonials, friendlies and tour matches.

● Jock Lauderdale and Garry Thompson achieved their totals without scoring a hat-trick.
● Ian Wallace reached his total without scoring any goals in the FA Cup.

HIGHFIELD ROAD FIRSTS

FIRST MATCH
v. Shrewsbury Town. Birmingham & District League. Sep. 9, 1899. Att. 3,000. Result W 1-0.
FIRST HAT-TRICK
Harry Walker. v. Aston Villa Res. B'ham & District League. Dec. 23, 1899. Att. 800. Result W 3-0.
FIRST LEAGUE MATCH
v. Tottenham Hotspur. Division Two. Aug. 30, 1919. Att. 16,500. Result L 0-5.
FIRST FLOODLIT MATCH
v. Queen of the South (Friendly). Oct. 21, 1953. Att.16,923. Result D 1-1.
FIRST SUBSTITUTE
Dietmar Bruck. v. Manchester City, on for Ron Farmer. Sep. 4, 1965. Att. 29,403. Result D 3-3.
FIRST CLOSED CIRCUIT TV PICTURES
v. Cardiff City (a). Oct. 6, 1965. Att. 10,295. Result W 2-1. *Attendance in Cardiff: 12,639.*

FIRST SUNDAY MATCH
v. Derby County. FA Cup R.4. Jan. 27, 1974. Att. 41,281. Result D 0-0.
FIRST ALL-SEATER MATCH
v. Manchester United. Division One. Aug. 29, 1981. Att. 19,329. Result W 2-1.
OTHER EVENTS STAGED AT HIGHFIELD RD
Highfield Road has staged Rugby Union, women's football, boxing, motor cycle football (in the 1920s), beer festivals, functions, a Billy Graham religious meeting, weddings, wedding fayres, fashion shows and an Abba night.

HIGHFIELD ROAD TIMELINE
Here's a short history of Coventry City's former home ground. Other notable football events in *italics*
1899 Coventry City move to their new ground at Highfield Road. A grandstand housing 2,000 is built. Known as the John Bull Stand, it costs £100 and will last 37 years.

1902 The six-yard box (goal area) replaces the two arcs or kidney-shaped area. The penalty area replaces the 18-yard line across the width of the pitch.

1908 Coventry City are admitted to the Southern League.

1910 The funds from a run in the FA Cup help the club pay for a new barrel-roofed stand opposite the Main Stand, which costs £1,000.

1919 Coventry City are elected to the Second Division of the Football League.

1922 The Kop or East Terrace is built up, using waste from the relaying of the city's tram track.

1925 New offside law introduced.

1927 The West Terrace is covered with a roof stand bought from the rugby ground at Twickenham, for £2,000. This provides cover for 11,000 people behind the goal.

1936 The club celebrates promotion back to Division Two with a replacement for the John Bull Stand. The £14,000 cost is raised from an appeal fund.

1936 In November the club purchases the freehold of the ground for £20,000. The money comes from a loan to the club by Sir John Siddeley.

1937 The "D" is added to the penalty area.

1938 The East Terrace is extended upwards with the addition of a lattice board section, known as the "Crows Nest." The capacity of the ground has now reached 40,000.

1939 Numbering of players introduced.

1940 The Second World War devastates the city of Coventry and on November 14th. three German bombs hit Highfield Road. The bombs leave craters in the pitch, but the stands are undamaged.

1951 White ball brought into official use.

1956 First league fixture under floodlights, March 19th. v. Southend United.

1957 The pole lights are replaced by tower or

Highfield Road becomes Britain's first all-seater stadium in 1981

pylon floodlights. The improved lights illuminate a friendly against Third Lanark. Costing £15,000, the lights have been paid for with money raised by the Supporters Club.

1963 The construction of the new Sky Blue Stand commences, with the building of the two end wings either side of the original 1910 barrel-roofed stand.

1963 The pitch slope is levelled. The supporters club raise £13,000 for the job, which has to correct a slope of six feet from one side to the other and eight feet from one corner to the other.

1964 The Sky Blue Stand is completed with a distinctive scallop shaped roof. A large proportion of the £120,000 cost is raised by the Supporters Club.

1964 An electronic scoreboard is installed at the Spion Kop End. Donated by the Coventry Evening Telegraph, it costs £3,000.

1965 *Substitutes allowed in league matches, one per team.*

1967 BBC Match of the Day visits Highfield Road for the first time for the Division Two game against Bolton Wanderers on March 11th Bobby Gould scores in a 1-1 draw.

1967 The West Stand is built to replace the old covered terrace. A double-deck stand, it costs £85,000 to build and can seat 3,200 in the upper tier.

1968 The Main Stand is gutted by a fire on March 16th The dressing rooms, club's offices, directors' box, press box and shop are all destroyed.

1968 Only four months, or 40 working days after the fire, a new Main Stand is completed at a cost of £150,000.

1973 12 luxury boxes are installed in the Main Stand in May.

1978 Fences are erected around the perimeter of the stands to separate the fans and the pitch.

1980 Undersoil heating is installed in the summer beneath the pitch.

1981 Highfield Road becomes the first all-seater stadium in Britain. The capacity of the ground drops from 36,500 to 20,600 and the fences are removed.

1981 *Three points for a win introduced by Football League.*

1985 The seats in the Spion Kop End are removed and the terracing is restored. The ground capacity rises back up to 26,000.

1993 *Squad numbers are introduced to league football.*

1994 The Spion Kop End is replaced with a new East Stand, which inludes bars and hospitality suites. The ground becomes all-seater again.

2005 Coventry City play their last league game at Highfield Road against Derby County on April 30th The Sky Blues win 6-2 and are safe from relegation from the Championship. Attendance 22,728.

HIGHFIELD ROAD
PRE-MATCH ENTERTAINMENT

Here is an example of pre-match entertainment in 1965 for the first match of the new season against Wolverhampton Wanderers:

SATURDAY AUG 21 1965
12.30 GATES OPEN
2.00 RADIO SKY BLUE
2.25 NETBALL MATCH
2.55 HILLMAN IMP, WON BY COVENTRY MAN IN LOCAL
"GOOD MANNERS" ROAD SAFETY COMPETITION, DRIVEN ROUND TRACK BY ROSEMARY SMITH.
3.15 KICK-OFF

● The attendance for the netball match between the Sky Blues ladies team and their Wolves counterparts is believed to be the biggest ever attendance for a women's netball match. The match was won by the Sky Blues side 20-3. The crowd of 40,000 stayed on to watch the football.

● Pre-match entertainment has included live music, military marching bands, trampolining, netball, the Royal Signals motor-cycle display team, and the RAF dog handlers.

HILL, BRIAN

Brian Hill remains today the youngest player to score for Coventry City. He was the club's youngest player when he made his debut, a record held for more than 40 years.

In addition, he also holds the unique record of playing in five divisions of league football plus Europe, all for Coventry City.

Hill was first spotted playing for the Nicholas Chamberlain school team in Bedworth as a centre forward.

He then played for Nuneaton schoolboys and the Birmingham County XI, joining the groundstaff at Coventry City in 1956. As he was the only groundstaff boy at the time, he was kept busy with jobs around the ground and had little time to train.

Nevertheless, he was given his debut on April 30, 1958 in an away match at Gillingham at the age of 16 years 273 days and scored in a 2-3 defeat.

Having given Hill an early start to his playing career, manager Billy Frith restricted him to occasional games over the next two seasons. Hill was also hampered by muscle strains which prevented a settled run in the side.

For the next four years Brian was played in all the forward positions. However, the club's new manager Jimmy Hill switched Hill to defence and he became a feature in the side. In 1962-63 he was almost ever present. A key figure in the Sky Blue era, Hill missed just six games in the Division Three Championship-winning season, 1963-64.

Injuries continued to interrupt Hill's consistency in the team line-up, but when available he was reliable and solid in defence. He was versatile and played in all the back positions or as a defensive midfielder when called upon. A quiet man off the pitch, Brian let his football do the talking.

Hill became a man-marking specialist, containing

Brian Hill's Testimonial

the forwards of the day, the likes of Geoff Hurst, Jimmy Greaves and George Best.

Following Coventry's promotion to the First Division in 1967, Brian continued to feature under manager Noel Cantwell. In the 1968-69 season he appeared no less than 31 times, including 20 consecutive games. It was an impressive achievement in what was also his benefit year.

Brian Hill's loyalty to the club was rewarded with a Testimonial match against Division Two Champions Derby County, in April 1969. More than 10,000 fans attended the 1-1 draw. Other events for Hill's benefit included a professional wrestling evening at the Leofric Hotel and a Vauxhall Viva car competition.

Over the next two season Hill appeared irregularly, but in the 1970-71 season, City played in the European Fairs Cup and Hill made a swansong appearance in the second round, home-leg tie, against Bayern Munich.

The Sky Blues won 2-1, going out on aggregate to the West German giants. It was almost Hill's last game for the club.

He played his very last match on December 26, 1970 against West Bromwich Albion in a 1-1 draw at Highfield Road. Over his career, Brian had played for Coventry in every position except goalkeeper.

In March 1971 Brian Hill went on loan to Bristol City and returned briefly to Coventry before transferring to Torquay United in October 1971. He made 49 appearances for the Devon side between 1971-73, scoring one goal, before returning to Warwickshire to play for Bedworth United. After retiring from football, Brian worked at Jaguar cars for 18 years.

More recently he was working for a bank and, despite an arthritic knee, keeping fit at the gym each day.
1958-71. 284 Apps. 8 goals.

HOME COLOURS
(continued from Sky Blue Heaven Vol I)
2002-03 Sky Blue shirt with navy trim, navy shorts
2003-04 Sky Blue shirt front & back, navy sleeves, navy shorts
2004-05 Sky Blue shirt, shorts and socks
2005-06 Sky Blue and white striped shirt, sky blue shorts, white trim

INDIVIDUAL SCORING IN ONE GAME
The following players scored more than a hat-trick for Coventry in a league or cup match, 1919-2005.

GOALS IN ONE GAME AT HOME
5 **Clarrie Bourton** v Bournemouth. Division 3(S)
Oct 17 1931 W 6-1.
5 **Cyrille Regis** v Chester City. League Cup R2 2nd leg
Oct 9 1985 W 7-2.
4 **William Paterson** v Doncaster Rovers. Division 3(N)
Sep 12 1925. W 4-0.
4 **Frank Herbert** v Watford Division 3(S).
Jan 1 1927 W 5-1.
4 **Billy Lake** v Bristol Rovers Division 3(S).
Mar 21 1931 W 5-1.
4 **Clarrie Bourton** v Mansfield Town. Division 3(S)
Dec 12 1931 W 5-1.
4 **Arthur Bacon** v Crystal Palace. Division 3(S)
Jan 6 1934 W 5-1.

4 **Clarrie Bourton** v Bristol City Division 3(S)
Apr 28 1934 W 9-0.
4 **George Lowrie** v Sheffield Wednesday Division 2
Apr 5 1947 W 5-1.
4 **George Lowrie** v Luton Town Division 2
Aug 23 1947 W 4-1.
4 **George Lowrie** v Bradford Park Avenue Division 2
Nov 8 1947 W 5-0.
4 **Jimmy Rogers** v Aldershot. Division 4
Sep 22 1958 W 7-1.
4 **Ken Satchwell** v Wrexham Division 3
Dec. 25 1959 W 5-3.
4 **Mick Ferguson** v Ipswich Town Division 1
Dec 1 1979 W 4-1.
4 **Steve Livingstone** v Sunderland League Cup R5 (R)
Jan. 24 1990 W 5-0.

INDIVIDUAL GOALS IN ONE GAME, AWAY
5 **Arthur Bacon** v Gillingham Division 3(S)
Dec 30 1933 W 7-3.
4: **Billy Lake** v Luton Town Division 2
Feb 19 1938 W 4-1.
4: **George Stewart** v Carlisle Utd Division 4
Feb 14 1959 W 6-1.

● Arthur Bacon's five goals in the game at Gillingham in 1933 were followed by four in the next match, at home to Crystal Palace. His haul totalled 14 goals in just five league games.

INTERNATIONAL APPEARANCES
Coventry City's most capped players. Caps with Coventry – first figure, Total caps in brackets.
Magnus Hedman (Sweden)   44   (58)
Gary Breen (Rep. Ireland)   33   (61+)

Peter Ndlovu (Zimbabwe)	26	(50+)
Roy Wegerle (USA)	21	(41)
Dave Clements (N.Ireland)	21	(48)
Ronnie Rees (Wales)	21	(39)
Terry Yorath (Wales)	20	(59)
Jimmy Holmes (Rep. Ireland)	17	(30)
Tommy Hutchison (Scotland)	17	(17)
Gerry Daly (Rep. Ireland)	15	(48)

+ indicates still playing.

● Roy Wegerle (USA) played for a World Stars XI (a squad of 30 players) against Russia in St.Petersburg in August 1994.

● Moustapha Hadji (Morocco) played for a FIFA World XI against South Africa in honour of Nelson Mandela in August 1999.

IRELAND INTERNATIONALS

The following players represented the Republic of Ireland:

Jackie Brown	2	(2)	1937
Jimmy Holmes	17	(30)	1971-77
Gerry Daly	15	(48)	1980-84
Ashley Grimes	2	(18)	1984
Phil Babb	9	(35)	1994
Liam Daish	3	(5)	1996
Gary Breen	33	(62+)	1997-02
Robbie Keane	9	(60+)	1999-00
Barry Quinn	4	(4)	2000
Lee Carsley	2	(29+)	2001
Graham Barrett	6	(7+)	2003-05
Michael Doyle	1	(1)	2004-

Caps while playing with Coventry, first figure. Total apps. in brackets. + indicates still playing.

Also Represented Eire:
Reg Ryan 16 caps *1950-56* City player 1958-61
Pat Saward 18 caps *1954-63* City Player-Coach 1963-67; Assistant Manager 1967-70
Noel Cantwell 36 caps *1954-67* Eire Manager, *1967-*

68. City Manager 1967-72
Colin Healy 1 cap (9+) *Celtic (on loan to City) 2002.*
Steve Staunton 102 caps *1989-02* City player 2003-05.

● Both Jackie Brown and Paddy Ryan also played for Northern Ireland.

● Graham Barrett scored on his international debut against Finland, as a substitute. He also scored on his first full appearance v. Jamaica, June 2, 2004 at The Valley.

● Robbie Keane with 24 goals is Ireland's all-time record goalscorer.

JONES, LESLIE

Leslie Jones

Welshman Les Jones starred in the Coventry frontline during the 1930s with a return of a goal every other game over five exciting seasons and is the eighth highest goalscorer in the history of the club. Sadly, his Coventry City story is also one of what might have been.

Born in Aberdare in 1911, he began his footballing career with his town team before moving to Cardiff City. He was capped for Wales against France in 1933 despite playing in Division Three(S). After impressing Coventry manager Harry Storer with his displays against City at Christmas 1933, Jones moved to Highfield Road for a £2,000 fee in January 1934.

He was an immediate success and linked with City's other frontmen Clarrie Bourton and Jock

Lauderdale. Jones scored ten goals but City just missed out on promotion, finishing second in the table. The next season Les caught fire scoring 27 league goals, which was one more than recognised centre-forward Bourton's total. The Bantams scored 86 goals but again missed out on promotion, finishing third.

In the next season 1935-36, it all came together as Coventry finished Division Three(S) Champions. Jones, a key figure in the side hit the target 20 times out of 102 goals, as City took the title.

The 1936-37 season in Division Two was one of consolidation in the higher league. In 40 appearances Jones hit ten goals and Coventry stabilised with a finish in eighth place. He was still very much at his peak as the following season showed.

Then manager Harry Storer shocked the City faithful by agreeing to sell Jones to Arsenal in November 1937. A player exchange deal was done, with the Gunners paying £2,000 plus Bobby Davidson.

The feeling was that Storer blew the club's chances of promotion to the top league. Coventry's loss was Arsenal's gain. Jones won a Division One Championship medal in his first season at Highbury.

During the Second World War, Jones played as a guest for many clubs including Coventry. Following the war he moved to Swansea Town as player-coach then moved to Barry Town in a similar capacity. He then returned to league football to scout for Brighton.

In June 1950 he had the honour of becoming Scunthorpe United's first Football League manager. Jones brought in some new men to the Old Showground, many of who were fellow-Welshmen. Other signings were former West Bromwich Albion and England International Wally Boyes and Ted Gorin, who became the club's leading goalscorer.

Jones proved to be a shrewd tactician and Scunthorpe's final league position of 12th was the best of all the four newcomers to the two Third Divisions. Relationships between some Board members and the manager turned sour towards the end of the season and as a result of criticisms, Jones resigned in the summer of 1951. He left football afterwards. Les Jones died in Brighton in the early 1980s.
1934-38. 144 apps. 74 goals.

KIRK, ROY

Roy Kirk was a solid defender during the difficult 1950s and was an automatic choice in the side for seven seasons. Sadly for Kirk, City were languishing in Division Three(S) and for a year in Division Four, during his time at the club.
Born in Bolsover, Derbyshire, Roy Kirk began his football career for the local colliery side before joining Luton Town.

He moved to Leeds United in 1948 where he was understudy to John Charles. Harry Storer signed Kirk from the Elland Road club in March 1952 for a £10,000 transfer fee. He played the last nine games of the Division Two season but couldn't save City from relegation to Division Three(S).

They made a good attempt at immediate promotion, but when Roy missed the last five games, the form deserted the side at the same time. In 1953-54 Kirk was ever-present and switched from centre-half to the left back position. He repeated his remarkable consistency the following season, but Coventry continued to be no better than a mid-table outfit.

Although he should be recognised as a loyal and reliable servant of the club, Roy Kirk is also remembered for some mishaps and a freak goal.

Against Leyton Orient in September 1954, he scored two own goals which were enough to earn the visitors a 2-2 draw at Highfield Road.

He made up for that with a freak goal only a few weeks later in an FA Cup tie at Northampton Town. Standing just outside his own penalty area, Kirk cleared the ball in the general direction of upfield. It flew the length of the pitch and over the head of the stranded goalie – ex-City man Alf Wood – into the net. The goal won Coventry the tie, 1-0.

In the third round, in January 1955, City had a classic cup battle with First Division side Huddersfield Town. They heroically drew 3-3 at Leeds Road but then lost the replay at home after extra-time. The turning point was Roy Kirk's penalty miss. It was Coventry's first spot kick of the season but Kirk's shot hit the post and Huddersfield went through 2-1.

Despite frequent changes in the management of the club, Kirk remained a constant and reverted to the centre half role in 1955-56. When Billy Frith became manager in 1958, Roy moved to the right-back position for a full season of 46 league games, allowing George Curtis to fill the central defensive position.

In September 1958, against Aldershot, Kirk had to go in goal when Jim Sanders broke his leg. The position didn't unduly worry him, and City won 7-1.

In 1959-60 Kirk lost his place to Don Bennett and in the summer of 1960 left Coventry to join non-league Cambridge United as player-coach.

In 1964 he became manager of the club. In May 1966, after two years in that role, he resigned over a policy matter. In June 1967 he joined neighbours Cambridge City, but resigned ten months later to run a pub in Peterborough. Roy Kirk died in 1983. 1952-60. 345 apps. 7 goals.

LAUDERDALE, JOCK

Jock Lauderdale's outstanding scoring ratio of a goal every three games places him as the tenth highest scorer in Coventry City's history. His achievement is the more impressive given that he was not a centre-forward but played at inside right and he never scored a hat-trick for City.

Scotsman John Lauderdale was born in 1908 in Dumfries. He played for Parkhead FC, Third Lanark, Stenhousemuir and Queen of the South before moving to English football with Blackpool in October 1929.

Coventry boss Harry Storer persuaded Lauderdale to move further south in the summer of 1931, although it meant dropping two divisions from First to Third. He hit the ground running, scoring a goal on his debut against Fulham in a 3-5 defeat on the opening day of the 1931-32 season.

Jock's inside forward play was the perfect support to centre-forward Clarrie Bourton. The newly formed partnership amassed no less that 69 goals between them that first season. Lauderdale scored 19 of those goals and he became an immediate favourite with the fans making the number eight shirt his own. City had done one of their best bits of business in signing the two front men.

The total outlay for the pair had been £1000.

Coventry pushed for promotion from Division Three(S) over the next four seasons with Lauderdale both skilful and hard working, contributing much to the cause. City just missed out on promotion in 1934 and 1935 and Jock began to find his place in the team challenged by Les Jones.

In 1935-36 City won the Division Three(S) Championship and although he was no longer an automatic selection for the side, Jock still contributed 11 goals in his 23 league games that season. The following season, Lauderdale was past his best and made just four appearances in Division Two.

During his time at Coventry City, Jock Lauderdale attracted the interest of other clubs keen to sign him, including Liverpool.

He had plenty of offers when he was allowed to move on and chose Northampton Town so that he could remain living in Coventry. City collected a £1,700 fee for his services in November 1936. He later played for Nuneaton Borough and during the war returned to Coventry to make nine guest appearances.

After the war, he worked for Armstrong Siddeley and continued to live in the city. He died at the early age of 58 in 1965.
1931-37. 182 apps. 63 goals.

LEAGUE CUP

The League Cup is, on the face of it, one of those competitions that Coventry City should have excelled in. Yet City have largely under-performed in this particular knockout. Since the competition was introduced in the 1960-61 season, City have

Garry Thompson in action for City in the first leg of the League Cup Semi-Final at Highfield Road in 1981

never reached the final, despite being a top-flight club for most of that time.

The Sky Blues have reached the League Cup Semi-Final on two occasions, in 1981 and 1990.

In 1981 City faced West Ham, then a second division side, but one which contained a fair sprinkling of classy players, including Trevor Brooking, Frank Lampard snr, Alan Devonshire and Billy Bonds.

The first leg was at Highfield Road and it got off to a dreadful start for City, with a Les Sealey error and a Garry Thompson own goal gifting the Hammers a 2-0 lead with only 35 minutes gone.

But a youthful Sky Blues side showed true character to stage one of the finest comebacks in the history of Coventry City. Garry Thompson struck twice and Gerry Daly was also on target as City scored three goals in the last 19 minutes of the game to give Gordon Milne's side a slender advantage for the second leg in east London.

Sadly, it proved insufficient. On a highly-charged night at Upton Park, City's youth and inexperience finally told as City capitulated in the last half hour. A goal from Paul Goddard after 61 minutes made the scores level.

And just when the massive and vocal Sky Blue Army thought that extra time was on the cards, Jimmy Neighbour popped up a minute from time to give the home side a 2-0 win on the night, making it 4-3, on aggregate.

1980-81
1st Leg Coventry City 3, West Ham United 2. January 27, 1981. Att. 35,468. Scorers: Thompson (2), Daly.
Team: Sealey, Thomas, Roberts, Blair, Dyson, Gillespie, Bodak, Daly (Jacobs), Thompson, Hateley, Hunt.

2nd Leg West Ham United 2, Coventry City 0. February 10, 1981. Att. 36,551.
Team: Sealey, Thomas, Roberts, Blair, Dyson, Gillespie, Bodak (Jacobs), Daly, Thompson, Hateley, Hunt.
Aggregate score: Coventry City 3, West Ham United 4.

In 1990, City again fell short by a single goal. Despite losing 3-1 at Grimsby in the opening tie of the campaign – City recovered with a 3-0 victory in the home leg – John Sillett's men progressed smoothly, scoring a 5-0 win over Sunderland in the quarter-final.

Steve Livingstone scored four goals in that match and got his fifth of the competition in the semi-final, first leg, against Brian Clough's Nottingham Forest at the City Ground.

His strike was an equaliser in the 72nd minute. Nigel Clough had put Forest ahead from the spot in the 37th minute after the referee penalised Cyrille Regis for hand-ball when it clearly struck his

leg. Livingstone's goal provided hope but City's joy proved short-lived when Sky Blues old boy Stuart Pearce restored Forest's lead 11 minutes from time.

Still, City had the perfect opportunity to go through with home advantage two weeks later but could not find a way past the Forest defence. The second leg ended goalless and Forest went through to the final.

1989-90
1st Leg Nottingham Forest 2, Coventry City 1. February 11, 1990. Att. 26,153. Scorer: Livingstone.
Team: Ogrizovic, Borrows, Downs, Dobson, Kilcline, Peake, Gallacher, Gynn, Regis, Livingstone, Smith.

2nd Leg Coventry City 0, Nottingham Forest 0. February 25, 1990. Att. 25,500.
Team: Ogrizovic, Borrows, Downs, Speedie, Kilcline (Dobson), Peake, Gallacher (Drinkell), Gynn, Regis, Livingstone, Smith.
Aggregate score: Nottingham Forest 2, Coventry City 1.

LOAN PLAYERS

Coventry City were the first club to officially loan a player to another Football League club, when John Docker was loaned to Torquay United in July 1967. He made five appearances for the Devon side, which turned out to be his only games in league football.

Since relegation from the Premiership in 2001, loan arranging has played a major role in shaping the side. Whether that is a good thing or not is a subject for debate. The list below is a reminder of the names that have come and for the most part, gone, since the summer of 2001.

PLAYERS LOANED TO COVENTRY CITY SINCE 2001
2001-02 Lee Mills (Portsmouth), Tim Flowers (Leicester City), Colin Healy (Celtic), Horacio Carbonari (Derby County), Paul Trollope (Fulham)

2002-03 Richie Partridge (Liverpool), Gary Caldwell (Newcastle United), Brian Kerr (Newcastle United), Craig Hignett (Blackburn Rovers), Dean Holdsworth (Bolton Wanderers), Jamie McMaster (Leeds United), Matt Jansen (Blackburn Rovers), Vicente Engonga (Real Mallorca), Juan Sara (Dundee), Ben Williams* (Manchester United)

2003-04 Stephen Warnock (Liverpool), Yazid Mansouri (Le Havre), Johnnie Jackson (Tottenham Hotspur), Peter Clarke (Everton), Martin Grainger (Birmingham City), Courtney Pitt (Portsmouth), Bjarni Gudjonsson (vfl Bochum), Eric Deloumeaux (Aberdeen), Brian Kerr, (Newcastle United), Sebastian Olszar (Portsmouth).

2004-05 Eddie Johnson (Manchester United), Andy Marriott* (Colchester United), Luke Steele (Manchester United), Dean Leacock (Fulham), Matthew Mills (Southampton), Rohan Ricketts (Tottenham Hotspur), Florent Laville (Bolton Wanderers), Richard Duffy (Portsmouth), Christian Negouai (Manchester City), Ian Bennett (Birmingham City), Lloyd Dyer (West Bromwich Albion), Shaun Goater (Reading)
Club loaned from in brackets.
*Did not make any appearances for Coventry City.

Mackay, Don

Don Mackay

Photographic records confirm that Don Mackay was briefly the boss at Coventry City. He didn't manage a complete season and was in charge for less than two years.

In his playing days Scotsman Mackay had been a goalkeeper for Forfar Athletic, Dundee United and Southend United. He coached at Bristol City during the mid-1970s. In 1980 Mackay moved back to Scotland to manage Dundee, winning promotion to the Premier League in his first season. After three years he left Dundee and in 1983 made a strange move to Denmark to manage Norlesundy.

Bobby Gould was manager of Coventry City when in September 1984, he remembered his old friend from their Bristol days; he brought Mackay back from the Danish wilderness to be his assistant at Coventry City. Mackay had only been with the club for three months when Gould was sacked.

The Boxing Day defeat to Luton by 2-0 sealed Gould's fate. Mackay took over initially as caretaker-manager on December 28th. His first match in charge a day later was a 2-1 home defeat to West Ham, but the next game saw an improvement as City gave Stoke City a 4-0 beating.

The new man enjoyed a brief flurry of decent results, including away wins at Manchester United and Newcastle United. After seven games as acting manager, Mackay was handed the job proper.

Striker Terry Gibson was in sparkling form, while the defence found resolve.

Then the honeymoon period came to end at Easter. A flu bug hit the club and three matches were postponed, with the result that when City resumed playing, they were in a bottom three position in the league. A classic Sky Blues dilemma to avoid relegation was inevitable. By May, the club would need to win all three remaining games to ensure safety. No other permutation would do.

First City scraped a 1-0 win at relegated Stoke, with Stuart Pearce hitting the winner from the penalty spot. Next up were Luton and, with the score 0-0 with six minutes to go, Coventry were facing the drop.

Hero of the day was Brian Kilcline whose volley was deflected for the winning goal. In the third and last game, Mackay's men had to beat newly crowned Champions and Cup Winners' Cup winners, Everton. They did it in style by a 4-1 scoreline. Cyrille Regis scored twice and Coventry were safe.

Mackay prepared for season 1985-86 with some optimism. He brought in two full backs who were destined to play a big part in Coventry's history – Brian Borrows and Greg Downs. At £80,000 and £40,000 respectively, they were good value.

However, Stuart Pearce had been sold to Nottingham Forest in the close season, and pre-season arguments with some of the players did nothing to suggest harmony in the camp. Trevor Peake, as captain, complained about facilities, hotel accommodation and a curfew imposed on the players, and was stripped of the captaincy.

The season proper started very badly with just one win in the first nine games. Mackay's tactic of playing Cyrille Regis as a target man did not work. Don Mackay's Scottish work ethic and emphasis on discipline were not a substitute for skill and tactics.

As the season wore on, City got worse and in January, a crowd of just 7,478 witnessed a 2-0 home defeat to Watford. The game followed the sale of Terry Gibson to Manchester United, but Gibson would still finish the season as City's top scorer.

The team went five games in March without a goal and, by the time Coventry lost 5-0 to Liverpool at

Anfield in April, they had gone eight games without a win. The day following the Liverpool humiliation, April 13th, Mackay resigned. City avoided relegation with two wins in their last three matches under caretakers George Curtis and John Sillett. An ironic footnote to 1985-86 was that the fans voted Trevor Peake as their Player of the Year.

Don Mackay was an uneasy occupant of the manager's chair at Highfield Road and had a rough ride in his relationship with the club's directors. He was thrust in charge of a club in financial difficulties, but most Coventry managers could claim that.

Mackay made some astute signings but he also signed players who fell short of the required standard. Most significantly, under his coaching, the team did not punch their weight. Only a year following his departure, largely the same squad won the FA Cup.

Following his time at Coventry, Mackay coached at Rangers before managing Blackburn Rovers, 1987-91. He was sacked 14 days into the 1991-92 season and moved to Fulham where he was manager between 1991-94.

He returned to the north of England to scout for Sheffield Wednesday. In 1996 Mackay became northern scout for Arsenal while at the same time running the Calf's Head pub in Worston, Lancashire. Mackay returned to Scotland where he managed Airdrie between 2000-01.

Assistant Manager: September 1984 – December 1984. Manager: December 1984 – April 1986. Managerial Stats: P67 W22 D12 L33 32.8% wins

McALLISTER, GARY MBE
Gary McAllister was born in 1964 in Motherwell, Strathclyde. He started his career with his home

club, making 70 appearances in four years. In 1985 he was in the Motherwell team that won the Scottish Division One Championship. He was spotted by Leicester City manager Gordon Milne who bought him in a double swoop along with Ali Mauchlen, considered the more valuable part of the £250,000 deal.

But it was McAllister who made the bigger impact, and he went on to become one of the finest midfield players in the country. His trademarks were an ability to pick out team-mates with precision passing, along with a pin-point striking of dead balls.

He enjoyed five years with the Foxes, hitting the net 52 times in 220 matches. While at Leicester, he made his International debut for Scotland in April 1990 against East Germany in a 1-0 defeat at Hampden Park. He was in the national squad for the World Cup in Italy that summer. In 1990 both Nottingham Forest and Leeds United showed interest in Gary before he moved to the Yorkshire club for a £1m. fee. Howard Wilkinson's side won promotion from Division Two and within two years were the final Division One Champions in 1992, before it became the Premier League.

McAllister and Gordon Strachan were team-mates in that successful side. In six years at Leeds, McAllister played 295 games, scoring 46 goals, including a hat-trick against City at Elland Road in October 1995.

Ron Atkinson lured McAllister to Highfield Road in the summer of 1996 for a club record fee of £3m. The move was a surprise to outsiders, but it demonstrated to Coventry City fans that the club meant business.

McAllister came to Coventry as Scotland captain after the drama of the England versus Scotland

match at Wembley, when he missed a penalty. Replays afterwards showed the ball moved slightly off the spot just before he hit it. In a Coventry shirt Gary McAllister took some time to settle in.

He suffered a setback with a long term knee injury in December 1997, which kept him out until the following October. And it was the 1999-00 season before Coventry supporters saw the best of him. Released from his defensive midfield duties his class shone through and he scored more frequently. In his fourth and last season McAllister was the highest scoring midfielder in the Premiership, the club's top scorer and voted Player of the Year.

Out of contract in the summer of 2000, he moved to Liverpool on a free transfer. Playing against Coventry in April 2001, he scored from a direct free kick in a 2-0 win for the Reds at Highfield Road. Macca didn't celebrate, knowing that the result meant relegation was a virtual certainty for his former club. In all he scored seven goals for his other clubs against Coventry City.

He was awarded an MBE in the New Year's Honours list of 2002.

Following the sacking of Roland Nilsson in April 2002, Coventry offered McAllister the chance to return as player-manager. After two successful years at Liverpool, his return was popular with many City fans but the size of the task facing him was not to be underestimated and, with no previous experience of management or coaching, it was a huge gamble by the board to appoint him.

The gulf between the Premiership and the division below, ever greater by the season, was not the ideal place for Macca to pull the strings. After a handful of games, Lee Hughes and David Thompson left for the Premier League. Few of the remaining squad of players were up to top league skill levels or speed of thought. The 2002-03 season needed a team that could grind out results and for a period City managed to do that. A good run in December and January saw them climb to sixth in Nationwide Division One, going ten games undefeated.

Then came the almost inevitable FA Cup humiliation. The shock 2-0 defeat at lowly Rochdale totally unhinged things and the team never recovered. In February they lost all four games. From the end of January to the end of the season they managed just one win in 17 games. They failed to score a goal in the last five games of the season. They finished in 20th position on 50 points, just two places above a relegation spot. City deployed 44 players, the most that they have used in a single season in the club's history.

Playing and managing, even with the experienced Eric Black as assistant manager, was proving a tough call for McAllister. By the start of the 2003-04 season, sights had been lowered and the best to be hoped for was a play-off place.

McAllister brought in players with promise in Stephen Warnock, on loan from Liverpool, along with Irishmen Graham Barrett and Michael Doyle who came on transfers from Arsenal and Celtic respectively.

A long sought-after target man was found in Dele Adebola. Andy Morrell arrived from Wrexham as the top scorer in the Football League, while the experienced Steve Staunton came from Aston Villa. Again, the squad had quantity with 36 men given a number, but did it have quality?

Gary McAllister

The new season started in the most tragic of ways. On the morning of the opening game at Watford, the home side's young player Jimmy Davis, on a season's loan from Manchester United, was killed in a car crash and the game was postponed. It meant that Coventry began the league season playing catch-up and again, they were far too inconsistent.

They won and lost almost in rotation. Worse still, the team's home form was terrible. Then another, non-football event, intervened. McAllister's wife Denise became seriously ill and he was allowed compassionate leave in December. Eric Black took over temporarily as manager. By the New Year, Gary was unable to continue at the club due to his personal situation and resigned as player-manager on January 12, 2004.

In all, McAllister was manager of Coventry City for a season and four months. He played his last game for the club against Sunderland on December 8, 2003 and scored from the penalty spot in a 1-1 draw.

Although he was under no illusions about the

MANAGERS RECORDS

Statistics for managers since 1967.

		P	W	D	L	%Wins
Noel Cantwell	1967-72	213	69	61	83	32.4%
Bob Dennison*	1972	12	3	2	7	25.0%
Gordon Milne	1972-81	436	150	121	165	34.4%
Dave Sexton	1981-83	96	30	24	42	31.2%
Bobby Gould	1983-84	72	21	18	33	29.1%
Don Mackay	1984-86	67	22	12	33	32.8%
George Curtis	1986-87	56	28	13	15	50.0%
John Sillett	1987-90	150	56	39	55	37.3%
Terry Butcher	1990-92	60	20	14	26	33.3%
Don Howe*	1992	20	3	8	9	15.0%
Bobby Gould	1992-93	59	18	19	22	30.5%
Phil Neal	1993-95	67	21	20	26	31.3%
Ron Atkinson	1995-96	74	19	28	27	25.6%
Gordon Strachan	1996-2001	214	70	54	90	32.7%
Roland Nilsson	2001-02	43	19	6	18	44.1%
Gary McAllister	2002-04	76	21	26	29	27.6%
Eric Black	2004	26	12	4	10	46.1%
Peter Reid	2004-05	31	10	8	13	32.2%
Adrian Heath	2005	3	1	0	2	33.3%
Micky Adams	2005-	17	5	5	7	29.4%

Roland Nilsson

*Caretaker/Acting Manager
Games as caretaker included within totals of managers who became full-time.
INCLUDED: League and Cup games, Europe and Charity Shield.

NOT INCLUDED: Optional cups e.g. Texaco, Full Members etc.
Mickey Adams statistics up to end of the 2004-05 season
See also Caretaker Managers

difficulty of the task when he returned to the Sky Blues, it was a tall order. Even an experienced manager would have struggled in the circumstances.

With hindsight, his wish to continue playing suggests that a coaching role Would have been his best move.But then, hindsight is a wonderful thing.
1996-2000: 140 apps. 26 goals. 2002-03: 60 apps. 12 goals. Total: 200 apps. 38 goals.
Player-Manager: May 2002 – January 2003.
Managerial Stats: P76 W21 D26 L29 27.6% wins

McDONNELL, MARTIN

Martin McDonnell was born in Newton-le-Willows in 1924. He played for Everton before serving in Normandy at the end of the war. Following the war McDonnell was briefly at Southport FC before Harry Storer, then Birmingham City manager, bought him in May 1947.

He played in the Blues' Second Division Championship side in 1947-48. In October 1949 Harry Storer, by then Coventry City manager, signed McDonnell for the second time, paying Birmingham a £10,000 transfer fee. In his six seasons at Coventry, McDonnell was a solid and reliable defender and hardly out of the side. He could play at either centre half or right back and was captain of the team for several periods.

However, he rarely crossed the half way line and was not on the scoresheet as a City player. Coventry went through a tough time in the 1950s and were relegated in 1951-52 from Division Two to Three(S). McDonnell stayed on as one of the few constants at the club while several managers came and went.

During the last part of the 1954-55 season, McDonnell lost his place in the side when Roy Kirk was switched from left back to centre half. In the summer of 1955 he moved to Derby County, signing for the third time for his old mentor, Harry Storer.

By then, McDonnell was 33 but played another three seasons at the Baseball Ground winning a Division Three (N) Championship medal in 1956-57. In 1958 he moved to Crewe Alexandra where he finished his football career.

McDonnell moved back to Coventry and, fittingly for a player who was safe as houses, became an estate agent in the city. His business advertised in the Coventry City match programme and also sold insurance. Martin McDonnell died of A heart attack in 1988 at the age of 63.
1949-55. 245 apps.

MASON, DICK
Born in Arley, Warwickshire in 1918, Richard Mason was a long-serving and loyal Coventry City man. For more than seven seasons he was a solid and dependable defender in the Bantams line-up. Dick Mason first played for his local miners' welfare side before joining Nuneaton Borough.

By the time he joined Coventry City in May 1946 he was 28-years-old. In September 1946 he became one of the oldest players to make his league debut.

The step up from non-league could not have been more dramatic. In a Division Two match against Newcastle United at St. James Park, a crowd of 55,313 were in attendance, the seventh biggest crowd ever to watch a Coventry City away league game. City lost 3-1, but would have a good season, finishing eighth. Manager Dick Bayliss selected Mason 26 times, playing him mostly as a wing half.

The next season, 1947-48, Dick was switched to the left back position by

Peter Reid

MANAGERIAL SHORT REIGNS
The shortest serving managers in Coventry City's history are:

19 games	George Raynor	(1955-56)	*resigned*
26 games	Eric Black	(2004)	*sacked*
28 games	Jesse Carver	(1955)	*resigned*
29 games	Dick Bayliss	(1945-47)	*died*
30 games	Harry Pollitt	(1919-20)	*sacked*
31 games	Peter Reid	(2004-05)	*mutual consent*
35 games	Jack Fairbrother	(1953-54)	*resigned*
43 games	Roland Nilsson	(2001-02)	*sacked*

For more short reigns, see: Caretaker Managers.

Billy Frith and he remained there as an automatic on the team sheet up to the 1953-54 season.

Mason was a consistent performer, solid in his tackles and good with his head. By the time he moved on, Dick was 36 and had registered more than 260 games for Coventry City.

He became player-manager of Bedworth Town in February 1955 and was there for three years before retiring.
1946-54. 263 apps. 2 goals.

MATTHEWS, REG

Goalkeeper Reg Matthews was the first Coventry City player to play for England and played for the club for five seasons in the 1950s. He remains Coventry's most capped England player.

In addition to his full caps, Reg made appearances for England B, England under-23, and a Football League representative side, all as a Coventry City player.

Born in Coventry in 1931, Matthews made his debut for the club in an away match at Southend United in March 1953, which City lost 1-0. The young Reg made ten appearances that season and a handful the next, as understudy to Peter Taylor.

For the 1954-55 season, Matthews was first choice keeper and in a turbulent time when the club had three managers during one season, Matthews was the one reliable and consistent feature.

Although City were a Division Three(S) side at the time, the outstanding Matthews came to the attention of England manager Walter

Winterbottom. Matthews made his England debut on April 14, 1956 in the massive occasion of the Scotland v. England International at Hampden Park, Glasgow, in front of 130,000 spectators. The match ended 1-1.

Matthews next game was England's first ever match against the mighty Brazil. At Wembley Stadium, the home side beat Brazil 4-2. Matthews went on to play further games for England against Sweden (0-0), West Germany (3-1), and Northern Ireland (1-1). In five games in the yellow jersey for his country, Matthews was never on the losing side. England team-mates at the time included another Matthews – Stanley, along with Billy Wright and Duncan Edwards.

Inevitably, bigger clubs became interested in Matthews and in November 1956, the same year as his England appearances, he moved to First Division Chelsea. The £22,500 fee was a world record for a goalkeeper at the time. However, after leaving Highfield Road, Matthews inexplicably never represented England again.

Reg played at Chelsea for five years, where one of his team mates was future Coventry City player and manager, John Sillett. He transferred to Derby County in October 1961 and stayed until 1968. In September 1964 he played in a Derby County side against Coventry in a 2-1 win for the Rams. In January 1967 he broke his jaw, which prevented him facing the Sky Blues in their Division Two promotion season.

In the summer of 1968 Matthews became player-manager of Rugby Town. By 1975 Matthews was working as the assistant-manager at Coventry Sporting at the time of their FA Cup run which provided him with a return to Highfield Road. The ground was the neutral venue for the second round match against Peterborough United in December 1975. Matthews continued to live in Coventry after his retirement.

Reg Matthews played a total of 116 games for Coventry City. Agile and athletic, he was a modern goalkeeper, ahead of his time in post-war football. Brave and courageous, he was a true sportsman and will be fondly remembered by all those who had the privilege of seeing him play. Reg died after a short illness at the age of 68, October 7, 2001. 1953-56. 116 apps.

MERCER, JOE OBE

A young Joe Mercer was told by Dixie Dean: "Your legs wouldn't last a postman his morning round." But Dixie was wrong. Despite his odd-shaped legs, Joe enjoyed a long playing career. He played for Everton between 1933-46 making 150 appearances.

He won a Championship medal in 1939 and five England caps while at Goodison Park before World War Two. After moving to Arsenal for a £7,000 fee, Mercer enjoyed post-war success. He won two more League Championship medals (1948 and 1953) and in 1950 the FA Cup.

The same year, he was voted Footballer of the Year. In 1954, following a broken leg, Joe finally retired from playing at the age of 39.

Mercer went into his first management job with Sheffield United. He moved on to Aston Villa where he began to have the same success as a manager that he had enjoyed as a player. His young side were known as "Mercer's Minors" and they went on to reach two FA Cup semi-finals, win a Division Two Championship and the League Cup. Mercer is probably best remembered as the man

Joe Mercer with Peter Shilton, coaching England

who resurrected the fortunes of Manchester City after joining them in the summer of 1965 to work with coach Malcolm Allison.

Under his ever-smiling managership, Manchester City were Second Division Champions in 1966 and League Champions in 1968. They won the FA Cup in 1969, the League Cup and the European Cup Winners Cup in 1970. Joe became one of only nine men to have won the League Championship as both a player and a manager.

These achievements, eclipsing those of the other Manchester team at the time, were sadly soon forgotten. The Maine Road club moved him upstairs with a cut in salary in 1972. Mercer felt badly treated by this and within days he was snapped up by Coventry City.

When Mercer joined Coventry in June 1972 as general manager, he wanted to bring in Jack Charlton as team manager, but City couldn't get him and Gordon Milne was appointed instead. The "M" men would enjoy a long stewardship of the Coventry dugout. While with the Sky Blues, Mercer stepped in as England caretaker-manager following the sacking of Alf Ramsey. Joe's England record is: Played 7. Won 3, Drew 3, Lost 1. (May-July 1974).

Don Revie was his full time successor in the post. In December 1974, Joe Mercer selected a team to represent the West Midlands against a Don Revie All Stars XI. The match was in aid of the Birmingham Lord Mayor's appeal for victims of the IRA bombings in the city. Joe chose three Coventry players in his squad of 18 – Carr, Stein and Hutchison.

The match ended 1-1 with goals from Gerry Francis and Tommy Hutchison. Hutchison was a success with his dazzling wing play and a large crowd of 25,833 attended.

In the summer of 1975, Mercer moved from general manager to the boardroom at Highfield Road, becoming a Director. Joe made sure that the club's youth development would benefit the club in years to come.

He was awarded an OBE in the New Year Honours list of 1976 for his services to football. The Sky Blues enjoyed a terrific 1977-78 season and Joe Mercer continued on the board of directors of Coventry City until he left the club in 1981 and retired. In total he had been with Coventry City for nine years, a longer period than he had served at Manchester City.

He returned to live on the Wirral in Cheshire and occasionally would watch his local team Tranmere Rovers. One of the greatest ever managers in English football and one of the most respected figures in the game, "genial" Joe Mercer died in 1990 at the age of 76.

General Manager 1972-75. Director 1975-81.

MILLION POUND PLUS

TRANSFERS

It's hard to believe now, but for a period in the 1990s and early 2000s, Coventry City were one of the biggest spending (and selling) clubs in Britain as this list of £1million-plus transfers confirms.

PLAYERS IN

£6m	Robbie Keane *Wolverhampton W*	Aug 1999
£6m	Craig Bellamy *Norwich City*	Aug 2000
£5m	Lee Hughes *West Bromwich Albion*	Aug 2001
£4m	Moustapha Hadji *Deportivo La Coruña*	Jul 1999
£3.3m	Viorel Moldovan *Grasshoppers Zurich*	Jan 1998
£3m	David Thompson *Liverpool*	Aug 2000
£3m	Gary McAllister *Leeds United*	Jul 1996
£2.6m	Robert Jarni *Seville*	Aug 1998
£2.5m	Gary Breen *Birmingham City*	Jan 1997
£2.5m	Lee Carsley *Blackburn Rovers*	Dec 2000
£2.1m	Mohammed Konjic *Monaco*	Jan 1999
£2m	Dion Dublin *Manchester United*	Sep 1994
£2m	Noel Whelan *Leeds United*	Dec 1995
£1.9m	Steve Froggatt *Wolverhampton W*	Oct 1998
£1.7m	Eoin Jess *Aberdeen*	Jul 1977
£1.5m	Liam Daish *Birmingham City*	Feb 1996
£1.5m	John Salako *Crystal Palace*	Aug 1995
£1.3m	Laurent Delorge *Ghent*	Oct 1998
£1.2m	Cedric Roussel *Ghent*	Jan 2000
£1.1m	Paul Telfer *Luton Town*	Jul 1995
£1m	Richard Shaw *Crystal Palace*	Nov 1995
£1m	David Burrows *Everton*	Mar 1995
£1m	Regis Genaux *Liège*	Aug 1996
£1m	Paul Williams *Derby County*[1]	Aug 1995
£1m	Darren Huckerby *Newcastle United*	Nov 1996
£1m	Youssef Chippo *Porto*	May 1999
£1m	Runar Normann *Lillestrom*	Jul 1999

PLAYERS OUT

£13m	Robbie Keane *Inter Milan*	Aug 2000
£5-7m	Chris Kirkland *Liverpool*[2]	Aug 2001
£6.5m	Craig Bellamy *Newcastle United*	Jun 2001
£6.5m	John Hartson *Celtic*[3]	Aug 2001
£5.7m	Dion Dublin *Aston Villa*	Nov 1998
£5.5m	Darren Huckerby *Leeds United*	Aug 1999

Darren Huckerby (left) and Ian Wallace (right)

£4.5m	George Boateng	Aston Villa	Jul 1999
£4m	Viorel Moldovan	Fenerbache	Jul 1998
£3.7m	Phil Babb	Liverpool	Sep 1994
£3.3m	Robert Jarni	Real Madrid	Aug 1998
£2.5m	Lee Hughes	West Bromwich Albion	Aug 2002
£2m	Noel Whelan	Middlesbrough	Aug 2000
£1.9m	Lee Carsley	Everton	Aug 2002
£1.5m	Kevin Gallacher	Blackburn Rovers[1]	Mar 1993
£1.5m	Peter Ndlovu	Birmingham City	Jul 1997
£1.5m	Cedric Roussel	Wolverhampton W	Feb 2001
£1.5m	Magnus Hedman	Celtic	Aug 2002
£1.2m	Ian Wallace	Nottingham Forest	Jul 1980
£1.2m	John Aloisi	Osasuna	Jul 2001
£1.1m	Calum Davenport	Tottenham H	Aug 2004
£1m	David Thompson	Blackburn Rovers	Aug 2002

[1] Part Exchange
[2] Final fee depending on apps
[3] Some of the fee went to Wimbledon

MONTY PYTHONS FLYING CIRCUS

Coventry City featured in more than one sketch in the legendary BBC comedy show Monty Python's Flying Circus. First there was the "Communist Quiz" sketch *(see: Sky Blue Heaven Vol I)*. A live version also appears in the movie "Live at the Hollywood Bowl" (1982), which has undoubtedly ensured that Coventry City is a household name in the USA.

Another mention of Coventry City is in the "Sportsview" sketch. The sketch was in the style of the BBC Grandstand programme, except the sport was wife-swapping.

Eddie Waring (Eric Idle) commentating on a unique version of rugby league, hands back to Frank Bough (Michael Palin) in the studio. "Just a reminder that on Match of the Day tonight you can see highlights of two of this afternoon's big games. Mrs Robinson v Manchester United and Southampton v Mr Rogers, a rather unusual game that. And here's a late result....Coventry City 0, Mr Johnson's Una 3. Coventry City going down at home there."

This second reference to the club in a Python sketch cannot be a coincidence. Painstaking research has revealed the reason. Both sketches were written by Eric Idle, a Wolverhampton Wanderers supporter. In the late 1960s and early 1970s, Coventry and Wolves were rivals and the cheeky chappie couldn't resist the chance to take a poke at the Sky Blues.

Even more Python – Coventry City links follow this short intermission...

Welcome back. Jimmy Hill appeared in the fourth and last series on television – as Queen Victoria. In a sports programme with a Queen Victoria theme, there is racing in which all the runners in the Queen Vic handicap are men dressed as the monarch.

Next Brian Clough (Eric Idle) analyses a Real Madrid player getting sent off for breaking wind in

Monty Python, and especially Eric Idle (centre), had a fixation with Coventry and the Sky Blues

the 43rd. minute. The ref had no option as the same player had pursed his lips earlier. Next the real Jimmy Hill dressed in a Queen Victoria head-dress is asked what he makes of it. "Well the referees really are clamping down these days. Only last week the Belgian captain was sent off for having a Sony radio cassette player. And Gonnerelli that huge Italian defender was sent off in Turin for having his sitting and dining room knocked through to form an open living area."

And now for something completely similar. In a sketch in Python's second series, involving a cricket match commentary with a drunken team of experts, one of them mentions a player named Plum Warner. Coincidence or deliberate? Les "Plum" Warner was a Coventry City player and who should be mentioning his name? Our old friend Eric Idle.

MORGAN, BILL

Bill Morgan had an association with the club that

lasted more than 20 years, first as a player and later as head trainer. He was spotted by Harry Storer playing for Mickley Colliery Welfare in Northumberland, the same side that another Coventry keeper, Jerry Best, had come from. Having signed in October 1931, Morgan made his debut for Coventry City in December 1932 at the age of 18.

He was given a chance at the start of the 1933-34 season, but after letting in three goals against Exeter City, he was dropped. It was not until March 1936 that he became first choice goalie, returning in a 4-0 win over Northampton Town. Morgan timed things perfectly, playing the last 12 games of the Division Three(S) Championship season. Up to World War Two he missed just two games.

During the war he joined the local Fire Service, playing for City and as a guest player for Leicester City and Nottingham Forest. In 1942, playing for Leicester at Filbert Street, he suffered a shoulder dislocation which eventually ended his career. Morgan attempted a comeback but it was not possible and he was forced to retire from playing at the age of 26.

The club kept him on in a coaching capacity at Highfield Road and he was made assistant trainer in 1946. Bill also looked after Modern Machines, a nursery side to Coventry.

At the time the youngsters included Reg Matthews and Peter Hill. In 1951 he became head trainer but after two years in that role, he left football to work for Standard Triumph at the Canley works. Bill Morgan retired in the late 1970s and died in 1993.
Bill Morgan has the best record for clean

Coventry City's Bill Morgan in action

sheets of any Coventry City goalkeeper, having kept the ball out of the net in 50 of his 150 league games.
1932-44. 156 apps.
Coach, Assistant Trainer, Trainer. 1944-53.

MOST LEAGUE DEFEATS

22	1919-20 Division 2
22	1924-25 Division 2 *relegated*
22	1927-28 Division 3(S)
22	1951-52 Division 2 *relegated*
22	1984-85 Division 1

MOST LEAGUE GOALS SCORED

108	1931-32 Division 3(S)
106	1932-33 Division 3(S)
102	1935-36 Division 3(S) *Champions*
100	1933-34 Division 3(S)

MOST LEAGUE GOALS CONCEDED

| 97 | 1931-32 Division 3(S) |
| 96 | 1927-28 Division 3(S) |

MOST PLAYERS USED IN A SEASON

44	2002-03 Nationwide Division 1
43	1919-20 Division 2
36	1927-28 Division 3(S)
36	2004-05 Coca-Cola Championship
35	2003-04 Nationwide Division 1
34	1951-52 Division 2 *relegated*
30	1992-93 Premier League

MOST POINTS SCORED

2 Points For A Win

| 60 | 1958-59 Division 4 *Runners-up* |
| 60 | 1963-64 Division 3 *Champions* |

MOST POINTS SCORED

3 Points For A Win

66   2001-02 Nationwide Division 1 *11th.*
65   2003-04 Nationwide Division 1 *12th.*

MOST LEAGUE WINS

24   1935-36 Division 3(S) *Champions*
24   1958-59 Division 4 *Promoted*

NAMES

Players called Tooth and Cramp were in the same Coventry City side in 1906-07. Tickle and Buckle appeared together between 1908-11. Ike Turner played for City (without Tina) between 1908-1910.

***

What do Rome and Coventry have in common? Answer, Seven Hills. City have had seven "Hills" over the years, playing or coaching at the club.

The first was Walter Hill who played in 1910 when the club were in the Southern League. A forward, he didn't exactly make a big impression. On his debut, City lost 0-5 at QPR and Hill was dropped. He waited seven months to play again but returned in a 0-6 hammering at Plymouth. In his third and last appearance they drew 1-1 with Millwall. Needless to say, he didn't score the Coventry goal and disappeared from the football scene.

After some 40 years without a Hill on the pitch, like buses, three came along at once. Peter Hill, Brian Hill and Ray Hill were, perhaps surprisingly, no relation. The trio were in the same side for the end of season match at Gillingham in April 1958.

Peter and Brian (making his debut) each scored in the 2-3 defeat. A commentators dream or a nightmare? *"Hill to Hill, to Hill, who scores!"* The threesome also appeared in two matches together in the 1958-59 season in away games at Shrewsbury Town and Southport.

There was a fourth player named Hill in the 1950s, James Hill, who again, was no relation. He is not to be confused with his namesake manager and chairman Jimmy Hill who arrived in 1961.

The seventh Hill is Dick Hill – you've guessed, still no relation – who was trainer with the club in the 1930s and 1940s *(see: Unsung Heroes)*. There was even a player called Denis *Uphill* in the 1950s. How fitting that there should have been a player so named at a club inextricably linked to "Uphill Struggles."

***

Tomas Antonelius is the only man to change his name while with the club. At the end of the 2000-01 season he was just plain old Tomas Gustafsson, but for the start of season 2001-02, the Swedish player insisted on being known as Antonelius. The change might have worked wonders for his social status, got him near the start of the phone book listings and who knows, even a place in the Roman Forum, but it didn't re-launch his football career. He played six more times for the club before leaving in February 2002, to join Copenhagen.

***

A popular surname in the 1990s was Williams. First there was striker John Williams, officially the fastest footballer in the country having won the Rumbelows Sprint Challenge at Wembley in April 1992. He scored just nine minutes into his debut against Middlesbrough in August 1992. (86 apps. 14 goals).

No less than three players named Paul Williams

followed him. First there was Paul A. who made two appearances in 1992 on loan from West Bromwich Albion. Next came Paul R. a full back signed from Stockport County in the summer of 1993.

He made 17 appearances over two seasons and moved on to Plymouth in 1995 in time for his namesake, Paul D. Williams, to join the side without complicating matters.

It was third time lucky as this "Willo" went on to be a favourite at Highfield Road for six seasons. (1995-2001. 199 apps. 6 goals) and was Player of the Year in 1995-96. He moved to Southampton in 2001 and later played for Stoke City.

***

"You what John?" might have been heard during the 2004-05 season when John, Johnson and Gudjonsson appeared in the same City side. Wood played along with Sherwood and the club were linked to signing a player named Twigg.

***

Not surprisingly, the most common name at the club is Smith. There have been 14 Smiths to play for Coventry City — so far: John and Billy (prior to World War One); Archie, Bernard, Charlie, David, David F., George, Horace, John, Kevan, Norman, Stan and Wilf.

NATIONALITIES

Players from a bewildering number of countries have played for Coventry City – and it all began longer ago than you might think.

Jose Bilbao and Emilo Aldecoa were both Basque refugees who played for City during World War Two. Aldecoa, an outside left, was the more successful of the two and went on to turn out 29 times for Coventry when competitive football resumed in 1946. He returned to play for Athletic Bilbao in 1947.

Two South Africans made their mark in the 1950s. In 1956, outside right Steve 'Kalamazoo' Mokone became the first black player to play for City and two years later, goalkeeper Arthur Lightening began his three-year spell at Highfield Road.

There was then a bit of a gap before Roger Van Gool arrived in 1980, blasting a trail for slightly disappointing Belgians that came to include the likes of Regis Genaux, Phillipe Clement, Laurent Delorge and Cedric Roussell. All had their moments but were ultimately a little wanting, though to be fair to Genaux, he did make the cardinal error of falling out with Gordon Strachan.

Martin Jol's stay in 1984 was also frustrating and City never got to see the best of the man who was destined to return 20 years later as manager of Tottenham Hotspur.

If the 1980s saw a sprinkling of Europeans arriving at Highfield Road, by the 1990s it seemed the

The Smiths: Wilf (left) and David (right)

entire world was beating a path to City's door. An array of Africans, North Americans and South Americans came and went.

Peter Ndlovu, from Zimbabwe, was discovered on a pre-season tour to that country in 1990 and went on to appear 196 times in a City shirt in all competitions (including substitute appearances), scoring 41 times.

Some foreign imports, such as diminutive dread-locked USA international Cobi Jones, caused more of a stir off the pitch than on it. Jones arrived in August 1994 and only stayed one season. He

Cobi Jones (left) and Peter Ndlovu (right)

made 25 appearances all told but managed to score just twice.

However he generated a small storm of publicity for Coventry, and himself, with a refreshing attitude to what he insisted on calling "soccer".

As the "Big Ron" era turned to the epoch of "Wee Gordon", players from all over the world came to Highfield Road, but many were so under-utilised it is hard to know why all the trouble was taken to

bring them half the way across the globe.

Some, like Ysrael Zuniga from Peru, the Hondurans Ivan Guererro and Jairo Martinez and Romanian international striker Viorel Moldovan merely became expensive bench-warmers. Others, like Ukrainian defender Alex Evtushok, revealed themselves very quickly as below the required standards.

Others still – Moroccans Mostapha Hadji and Youssef Chippo and, later, Mo Konjic – proved themselves worth the effort, although the Bosnian defender Konjic only really flourished after Strachan had departed.

When financial crisis at Highfield Road hit hard following relegation in 2001, the atmosphere changed.

The imports were no longer the big star internationals with equivalent reputations, but loan signings of a a far more obscure nature.

A string of foreign imports arrived in deals that often smacked of desperation. Vicente Engonga – perhaps the slowest player ever to wear Sky Blue – Juan Sara, Christian Yulu and Sebastian Olszar all made the briefest of appearances but were proof, perhaps, that in football as in life, you get what you pay for. Their names will, no doubt, pass into Sky Blue legend.

The players named below were not necessarily international players for that country. This is the complete list of foreign (i.e from outside the British Isles) footballers to play for Coventry City.

Algeria	Mansouri
Argentina	Carbonari, Sara
Australia	Filan, Aloisi, McMaster, Cooney

Belgium	Van Gool, Genaux, Clement, Delorge, Roussel
Bermuda	Lightbourne, Goater
Bosnia	Konjic
Brazil	Isaias
Cameroon	Suffo
Denmark	Johansen, Hyldgaard, Jorgensen[1]
France	Wallemme, Debec, Yulu, Arphexad, Deloumeaux, Laville, Negouai
Germany[2]	Kruszinski
Ghana	Lamptey
Honduras	Guererro, Martinez
Iceland	Gudjonsson
Italy	Gioacchini, Nuzzo
Jamaica	Hall, Lowe
Morocco	Hadji, Chippo, Safri
Netherlands	Jol, Kaiser, Boateng
Nigeria	Adebola
Norway	Soltvedt, Normann
Peru	Zuniga
Poland	Olszar
Romania	Moldovan
South Africa	Mokone, Lightening, Wegerle[3]
Spain	Bilbao, Aldecoa, Engonga
Sweden	Nilsson, Hedman, Gustafsson/ Antonelius
Trinidad & Tobago	John, Ince
Ukraine	Evtushok
Uruguay	Perdomo
USA	Jones
Yugoslavia	Avramovic
Zimbabwe	Ndlovu

[1] Jorgensen a Dane, earned caps for the Faroe Islands, due to his mother's place of birth.
[2] Dietmar Bruck was born in Danzig, Germany, but moved to Coventry at an early age and played for England Youth.
[3] Wegerle was born in South Africa but played for the USA.

●The record for the **most nationalities in one match** was set when Chelsea played Coventry City on January 4, 2000. The players involved represented no less than 14 different countries. They were: England, Scotland, Ireland, France, Belgium, Italy, Netherlands, Norway, Sweden, Spain, Morocco, Nigeria, Uruguay, and Brazil.

●The Sky Blues used players of **nine different nationalities** in one game when they played Leicester City on April 24, 1999. Starting line-up: Sweden (Hedman), England (Burrows, Williams, Shaw, Huckerby), Ireland (Breen, Quinn), Belgium (Clement), Scotland (Telfer), Australia (Aloisi), Netherlands (Boateng). Plus substitutes used: Italy (Gioacchini), Norway (Soltvedt).

●England International **Terry Butcher** was born in Singapore while his father served with the Royal Navy.

●Both **David Phillips** and **Wilf Smith** were born in Germany while their fathers served in the Army. Their parentage allowed Phillips to become a Welsh international whilst Smith played for the England U-23s.

●**Terry Springthorpe** and **Gerry Baker** played for the USA although they were British nationals.

●Coventry City were one of the first clubs to employ a foreign coach when Jimmy Hill took on Hungarian **Janos Gerdov** in 1962.

NEAL, PHIL

Phil Neal is the most successful footballer to have managed Coventry City. His playing career began at Northampton Town where he was a team mate of ex-Sky Blues men Dietmar Bruck and Trevor Gould. He made 209 appearances for the

Cobblers before joining Liverpool for a £65,000 fee in 1974.

From then on he was more or less ever-present at right back with the most successful club side in English football. He won a record number of eight League Championships, an achievement shared by only Alan Hansen and Ryan Giggs. He won the European Cup with Liverpool in 1977, 1978, 1981, 1984, (runner-up in 1985) and the UEFA cup in 1976.

Out of a total of 635 appearances, 417 were consecutive and he scored 60 goals. He is the only Liverpool player to appear in five of their European Cup Finals and the only player to have scored in more than one of them. He was capped by England 50 times.

In 1985 Neal felt he was the man to succeed Joe Fagan in the manager's job at Anfield, but he was overlooked and Kenny Dalglish was given the job. Phil became player-manager at Bolton Wanderers during the 1985-86 season.

Neal was at Bolton for more than six years in a period when they played in Divisions Three and Four. In 1989 they won the Sherpa Van Trophy. He left Bolton in 1992 but was not out of football for long, joining Coventry as Bobby Gould's assistant for the start of the 1992-93 season.

In September 1992, Neal was appointed as part-time assistant manager to England boss Graham Taylor.

When Bobby Gould resigned unexpectedly after a 1-5 defeat at Queens Park Rangers on October 23rd, 1993, Phil Neal was appointed caretaker-manager. He became full-time manager a month

Phil Neal

later. To most fans, Neal was an unknown quantity. In his time as Gould's number two he had kept a profile so low as to be almost invisible.

Soon after he was appointed it became clear that in terms of personality he was the direct opposite of Gould. Whereas Gould was bubbly and loved to talk, Neal shied away from the spotlight and was unwilling to communicate freely, either with the fans or the press. However, when Neal did speak publicly, he tended to make some sense.

At first he enjoyed success. His record for the remaining part of the 1993-94 season was good. Neal brought in three players from the lower leagues. Julian Darby from his old club Bolton, Ally Pickering from Rotherham and in particular, Chris

Marsden on loan from Huddersfield added some quality and solidity.

After a dip in the New Year – coinciding with a loss of form by striker Mick Quinn – results picked up again. City finished the season undefeated in the last seven games. This included a win to deny Blackburn the Championship, an away win at Chelsea and a draw at Manchester United.
The 11th place finish gave optimism for the 1994-95 season. However, following the World Cup in USA 1994, the Sky Blues sold central defender and Player of the Year, Phil Babb, to Liverpool.

The Irish International had gone up in value to £3.75m after outstanding performances in the States, but his departure would leave the defence weaker. With money to spend, Neal took the brave step of signing a little known reserve striker from Manchester United. The fee at £2m seemed excessive, but Dion Dublin hit the target 16 times in 31 games that season.

In due course it would prove to be one of the best pieces of business Coventry City had ever done, but it would be Phil Neal's successors in the dugout who would benefit the most from Dublin's acquisition.

Defensively, Neal brought in Steven Pressley from Rangers but he was out of his depth and would not fill Babb's boots.

The squad lacked strength in depth and Neal's tactics were soon found out by the opposition, with a too-predictable playing style. The philosophy appeared to be that the way to win matches, or at least not lose them, was to stifle the opposition.

The 11-match spell without a win in the middle of the 1994-95 season spelt the end for Neal, particularly when a new chairman, Bryan Richardson, took over the reins at Highfield Road. Richardson like John Poynton four years before, hankered after a glamorous name to manage City and on February 14th sacked Neal to bring in Ron Atkinson.

The bad run coincided with striker Dublin's absence through injury, which was unfortunate for Neal. Ironically, Neal's last match in charge was a victory, 2-0 at Crystal Palace thanks to goals from two of his signings, Cobi Jones and a fit-again Dion Dublin. He left the Sky Blues in reasonable shape.

It is likely that, had he stayed, Phil would have secured a similar end of season position to that which Atkinson achieved, but Richardson was determined to have his revolution.

Neal was not helped by his dour persona or indeed by the Channel 4 documentary *An Impossible Job* during Graham Taylor's England reign. One sequence in the programme, of the dugout during a game, made Neal out to be a gormless "yes-man", which was very unfair.

In contrast, Neal had displayed eloquence rare for footballers in another documentary some years earlier. Asked about the Liverpool manager Bob Paisley, in a retirement tribute for the BBC Sportsnight programme, Phil Neal described him as "having the face of one of those Capo de Monte figurines."

Few City fans shed a tear when Phil Neal went, but his record was significantly better than his successor, the flamboyant but over-hyped Big Ron and was on a par with that of Gordon

Strachan, even though Strachan had millions more to spend.

After leaving Coventry, Phil Neal managed Cardiff City briefly then moved to Manchester City as assistant manager to Steve Coppell. He became caretaker boss when Coppell left after just 32 days in charge, but he too left after a short time. Neal later had a spell at Peterborough United as assistant manager.

Nowadays he can be found back at Liverpool on matchdays as a hospitality host as well as on radio and TV.
Assistant Manager: August 1992–October 1993.
Manager: October 1993–February 1995.
Managerial Stats: P67 W21 D20 L26 31.3% wins

NETBALL
See: Highfield Road, Pre-Match Entertainment

NEUTRAL CLUB GAMES STAGED AT HIGHFIELD ROAD
The disappearance of more than one replay in the FA Cup, and of replays altogether in the League Cup, means that Coventry City's ground is unlikely to be used as a neutral venue in cup competitions ever again.

So here's a complete list of the occasions on which Highfield Road was reverberating to the sound of two sets of supporters, neither of them Coventry's. (Or in one case, none at all.)

1946 Northampton v Peterborough FA Cup R2 2nd Rep Dec 23 Att 3,164. Result 8-1.
1967 Hull City v Portsmouth FA Cup R3 2nd Rep Feb 6 Att. 18,448. Result 1-3.
Future City player Chris Chilton scored Hull's goal.
1969 Brighton & HA v Walsall FA Cup R2 3rd Rep Dec. 17. Att. 2,241. Result 1-2.

A ball-boy watches in an otherwise empty Highfield Road as non-league side Burton Albion take on Leicester City in an FA Cup tie replayed behind closed doors in January 1985

1975 Coventry Sporting v. Tranmere R. FA Cup R1 Nov. 22. Att. 4,565. Result 2-0.
1975 Coventry Sporting v Peterborough FA Cup R2 Dec 13 Att. 8,556. Result 0-4.
1978 Aston Villa v Crystal Palace Lge Cup R3 2nd Rep Oct 16 Att. 25,445 Result 3-0.
1980 Arsenal v. Liverpool FA Cup Semi-Final 3rd Rep May 1. Att. 35,335.Result 1-0.
1985 Burton Albion v. Leicester City FA Cup R3 Jan 9 Att. 0. Result 0-1.
Match ordered to be replayed at a neutral venue and behind closed doors by the FA after the Burton goalkeeper in original tie (at Derby's Baseball Ground) was struck by a coin thrown by someone in the crowd. The original tie ended 6-1 to Leicester.

NICKNAMES
These days, footballers' nicknames are drearily predictible and are usually arrived at by placing an 'o' or a 'y' on the end of their surname. Not so long ago, however, players were a mite more inventive

with the epithets they gave to their team-mates. Here are some of the more unusual nicknames which Coventry City players over the years have somehow acquired.

"Leggy"	Robert Turner
"Cute"	Frank Herbert
"Twinkletoes"	Ernie Toseland
"Toffee"	Ray Straw
"Kalamazoo"	Steve Mokone
"Plum"	Les Warner
"Iron Man"	George Curtis
"The Scoop"	Mick Coop
"Spider"	Chris Cattlin
"Harry"	Brian Roberts
"Snoz"	John Sillett
"Bugsy"	Brian Borrows
"Killer"	Brian Kilcline
"Flying Postman"	John Williams
"Sumo"	Mick Quinn
"Bulawayo Bullet"	Peter Ndlovu
"Snowy"	Noel Whelan
"Detonator"	Moustapha Hadji
"Cachete" (Big Cheeks)	Ysrael Zuniga
"Stan"	Steve Staunton

NILSSON, ROLAND

Swede Roland Nilsson came to the football world's attention in 1987 when he was a member of the IFK Gothenburg side that won the UEFA Cup.

They beat Dundee United 2-1 over two legs and the match featured another future Sky Blues man, Kevin Gallacher.

By the time Ron Atkinson signed him for Sheffield Wednesday for a fee of £375,000 in 1989, Nilsson was considered to be one of the best full-backs in the world.

He was then 26 years old and had five years at Hillsborough. In 1991 the Owls won the League Cup and in 1993 Nilsson appeared on the losing side of both the FA Cup and League Cup finals with Wednesday.

As an international, he played in the 1990 World Cup in Italy and was an automatic choice for Sweden in both the European Championships on home soil in 1992 and the World Cup in 1994 in the USA.

In May 1994 he left Sheffield Wednesday to return home to Helsingborgs where he played for three

Roland Nilsson

years as a part-timer. In the summer of 1997, on the verge of taking up a job in insurance full-time, Nilsson was encouraged by his former manager Atkinson to make the move back to English football and sign for Coventry City. The fee was a bargain £200,000 and Nilsson signed a two year contract.

In two Premiership seasons Roland Nilsson was a class act. Fitter than most men ten years younger, he never suffered for being a predominantly right-footed player.

He made an impressive 39 appearances in 1997-98 and the Sky Blues finished a respectable 11th in the table. The following season Roland again set the example for the way the game of football should be played. As commentator Martyn Tyler said, "he turned playing in what could be described as the unattractive position of right back into an art form."

At the end of the 1998-99 season, the tributes for Nilsson as a player and as a man were unprecedented. There was unanimous praise from everyone at the club as Nilsson bid farewell. Roland moved back to Helsingborgs to become Director of Football, with a plan to retire from playing after Euro 2000.

It was not the end of the story, however, though in retrospect Roland may well wish that it were. In March 2001 he was persuaded to return to Coventry by Strachan. Although he was to fulfil a coaching role, he was still registered as a player. Unfortunately, City were relegated just two months later.

Life in the Nationwide First Division started badly and after an embarrassing home defeat to Grimsby Town in September, Strachan left the club. Nilsson was put in charge as caretaker-manager. In his first game Coventry won a League Cup tie at Peterborough on penalties after a 2-2 draw. In the league he had a dream start, with wins at Sheffield United and at home to both Manchester City and Portsmouth.

Roland soon brought back into the side players that Strachan had abandoned. The likes of Laurent Delorge and Jairo Martinez seized the chance and got on the scoresheet. Roland dropped himself from the team and would not appear as a player for some six months.

In his first full month as caretaker-manager, Nilsson won the Manager of the Month Award for October, and the job was made full-time. City were top of the table on October 27th and the whole atmosphere at the training camp markedly improved.

Nilsson assigned academy director Richard Money and scout Ray Clarke as his assistants and despite some inconsistency, City were looking good for a play-off place. In January, the vastly experienced Jim Smith was brought in as assistant manager. In February 2002 they won four in a row including a 6-1 win at Crewe Alexandra. As late as March 24th City were fifth in the table with just six games to go.

It all fell apart. A 3-0 defeat at Watford started a terrible run.

The disastrous conclusion was summed up in the away game at Preston. Nilsson returned to the line-up but he simply witnessed at close-quarters a side losing their way big-time. The 4-0 defeat was a humiliating display of such ineptitude that an irate fan ran on to the pitch and accosted goalkeeper Magnus Hedman.

Despite a highly creditable record of 19 wins in 43 games, the newly installed chairman Mike McGinnity wasted little time in sacking Nilsson just before the end of the season.

When the team faltered with the end in sight, Nilsson had been unable to restore their winning ways, although many fans saw Nilsson as the board's scapegoat. A major factor in the decline must have been Jim Smith.

Brought in by the board as the hard man to dish out some rollickings, he probably stirred things up too much. The team spirit vanished from the squad.

He was also instrumental in bringing in two loan players who were disasters – Horacio Carbonari and Paul Trollope.

The Sky Blues collected just one point from the last seven games of the season and ended in 11th position. City's disciplinary record was also a factor in their late collapse. City picked up no less than seven red cards in away games and committed the most fouls of any team in the league, an average of 15.5 per game.

One of the nicest men in football, Roland Nilsson won nine Sweden caps while with Coventry City out of a career total of 116. He became manager of Gais in Sweden on November 17th 2003. 1997-99. 69 apps 2001-02. 10 apps. Total 79 apps. Player-Manager: September 2001– April 2002. Managerial Stats: P43 W19 D6 L18 44% wins

NORTHERN IRELAND INTERNATIONALS
The following Coventry City players represented Northern Ireland. Caps while playing with Coventry – first figure. (Total apps. in brackets)

Jackie Brown	4 (10)	1936-38
Norman Lockhart	3 (8)	1950-52
Hubert Barr	2 (3)	1962-63
Willie Humphries	10 (14)	1962-64
Dave Clements	21 (48)	1965-71
Michael O'Neill	2 (31)	1996-97

Also Represented Northern Ireland:
Reg Ryan 1 cap - *West Bromwich Albion 1950*. (City player 1958-61).
Tommy Casey 12 caps - *Newcastle United, Portsmouth 1955-59*. (City First Team Coach 1972-75)

●Barr and Humphries were capped together against England as Coventry City players, in October 1962 at Windsor Park, Belfast. Barr scored the Ireland goal in a 1-3 defeat.

●Jackie Brown was capped by both Eire and Northern Ireland while a Coventry City player. Reg Ryan also played for Eire.

●Dave Clements was player-manager of Northern Ireland between March 1975- March 1976, whilst a player for Everton.

OCCUPATIONS
Jobs, trades or qualifications before playing football:

Electrician	Ray Graydon, Stuart Pearce
Shipyard Engineer	Colin Dobson *See: Unsung Heroes*
Miner	George Curtis, Neil Martin
Gravedigger	Ernie Hunt
Policeman	Steve Ogrizovic
Accountant	Andy Williams
Economics Graduate	Dave Bamber
Postman	John Williams
Financial Adviser	David Busst
Train Driver	Mo Konjic
Ice Hockey Player	Tomas Gustafsson *Swedish National League 2nd Division*

OLDER PLAYERS
Three players over the age of 37 appeared in the same season, during 2002-03. Gary McAllister, Steve Walsh and Vicente Engonga were the three 'senior' men. However, they did not all appear in the same side, at the same time.

***

Gordon Strachan was 40 years, two months, 24 days old when he last played for Coventry City against Derby County on May 3, 1997. He remains the oldest outfield player to appear in the

Tommy Hutchison

Premiership for any club.

***

An even more mature player to appear for the club is goalkeeper Steve Ogrizovic, who was 42 years, seven months, 22 days old when he made his farewell appearance. Oggy's 601st and last game was on May 6, 2000 against Sheffield Wednesday. Oggy is the second oldest Premier League player after goalkeeper John Burridge, who was 43 years, five months, 11 days old when he played for Manchester City in 1995.

***

Alf Wood is the oldest Coventry City player. Wood had retired from playing and was on the coaching staff when he was obliged to step in and cover for the injured Jim Sanders during the 1958-59 season.

Wood kept four clean sheets during his return spell and even saved a penalty in a 2-0 win over York City. Alf was 43 years, 207 days old when he made the last of 12 appearances in an FA Cup tie against Plymouth Argyle on December 7, 1958. Coventry lost the match at Highfield Road 3-1. Wood continued as trainer with the club until he lost his job in 1961 when there was a wholesale clearout of backroom staff after the appointment of Jimmy Hill as manager.

***

In post war English league football, Alf Wood is the fourth oldest player to appear, after Sir Stanley Matthews (50 years, five days), Peter Shilton and Dave Beasant. Following Alf Wood, the next oldest Football League player is ex-City star Tommy Hutchison, who was 43 years, 172 days old when he last played for Swansea City in 1991. Hutchison returned to Highfield Road in 2005 to play in the Michael Gynn testimonial at the age of 57. He may well be the oldest player to appear in an organised (albeit non-competitive) game at Coventry City. He rolled back the years and played for 60 minutes.

OLD FOES

The following are a list of defunct or former league clubs who Coventry City have played League games against since 1919.

Aberdare Athletic
Accrington Stanley
Aldershot
Ashington
Barrow
Bradford Park Avenue
Durham City
Exeter City
Gateshead
Halifax Town
Leeds City
Merthyr Town
Nelson
New Brighton
Newport County
Southport
South Shields
Thames
Wigan Borough
Workington Town
York City

OLYMPICS

Coventry City signed a player with an Olympic Gold medal when they signed Ted Hanney in November 1919 from Manchester City. Hanney had gained his honour at the 1912 Olympics in Stockholm, where he represented Great Britain in the football tournament. The British team were a combined English/Scottish side. They had also won the Olympic title four years earlier in 1908. Ted Hanney, a centre-half, was brought to Highfield Road for a huge transfer fee for the time of £2,000. He played a season and a half for City before moving to Reading. (36 apps. 1 goal)

***

George Raynor, manager of Coventry City in 1956, had previously been coach of the Sweden team that won the Gold Medal at the 1948 London Olympics and Bronze at the 1952 games. Raynor was at Highfield Road just over a year, joining as assistant to Jesse Carver in June 1955.

He was manager of City between January and June 1956, but he left in November 1956, having been demoted to chief coach. He returned to Sweden, and took over for his second spell in charge of the Sweden national side. It was to be Coventry's loss. (see: World Cup.)

***

Hubert 'Hugh' Barr, City inside forward, was in the Great Britain football squad at the 1960 Olympic Games in Rome. He played in three games. Jimmy Hill brought Barr to City in June 1962, from Linfield.

He played for Coventry between 1962-1965, and was also a full international for Northern Ireland. Barr scored a goal against England in 1962, the first City player to do so. Hugh left City in January 1965, to join non-league Cambridge United. During his time at City he was a part-time professional,

Coventry City Olympian: Hugh Barr (left) with Jimmy Whitehouse launching City's first ever Sky Blue kit in

also working as a teacher. He continued teaching full-time on leaving football.

***

Other players to have played in the Olympics and for Coventry are Roland Nilsson who played for Sweden in the 1988 games in Seoul; Nii Lamptey who was in the Ghana side that won Bronze at the 1992 games in Barcelona; John Filan represented Australia, also in Barcelona; Jairo Martinez and Ivan Guerrero played for Honduras in the Sydney Olympics in 2000.

***

The Olympics connection came fully up to date

when City signed Gold Medal winner Patrick Suffo in the summer of 2003.

The Cameroon international had represented his country in the 2000 Olympics at Sydney. Cameroon won the football Gold medal at the games, defeating Spain in the final. The sides were level at 2-2 after normal play. The "African Lions" went on to win on penalties 5-3.

***

Tenuous Olympic link: Ian Brightwell, who played just one game for Coventry City, is the son of Ann Packer and Robbie Brightwell. Mum Ann Packer won Gold at the 1968 Mexico Olympics in the 800 metres while father Robbie won a Silver at the same games, in the relay team.

ONE GAME WONDERS
Continued from Sky Blue Heaven Vol I
Sean Cooney 2002-03. 1 app. (sub.) *Left at the end of 2004-05 season.*

OVERSEAS GAMES
They do like a foreign trip at Coventry City. This section lists individual matches played abroad, *not* part of a summer tour. Therefore these overseas games were squeezed in mid-season or played at the end of season. *See: Summer Tours, for even more foreign outings.*

v Dutch XI April 6, 1932. Result W 3-0. Scorers, Cull, Lauderdale, Bourton. *The Club's first-ever overseas match. At Sparta Stadium, Rotterdam. A party of 12 players travelled. The players returned by ferry and suffered from seasickness on their return across the North Sea. They went directly from Harwich docks to play a league game at Norwich and blamed the seasickness they suffered, along with some injuries, for their 6-2 defeat.*

v Onteniente (Spain) May 24, 1964. Att. 2,000. Result W 5-2. Scorers: Hudson, Farmer, Hill B., Humphries, Smith. *End of season friendly near Valencia against a lower league side. The players' wives came along for*

Jimmy Hill and the Sky Blues departing for Spain in style in May 1964

this trip. *A proposed second game against nearby Gandia was cancelled.*

v Tunisia XI May 12, 1971. Result 2-2. Scorers: Rafferty, Alderson. *End of season friendly played in Tunis.*

v Olympiakos (Greece) February 29, 1972. Att. 10,000. Result W 1-0. Scorer: Billy Rafferty. *At Spiyros Louis, Athens. Mid-season away friendly.*

v Norrköping (Sweden) May 22, 1973. Result W 3-2. Scorers: Stein (2), Dugdale. *End of season away friendly.*

v Capdepera (Spain) May 26, 1973. Result W 5-0. *A*

second game abroad in a week. The opposition were a minor team on the east coast of Majorca.

v Saudi Arabia XI December 6, 1976. Result D 1-1. Scorer: Ian Wallace. *Mid-season away friendly. Played in Riyadh on an astroturf pitch.*

v Malta XI November 13, 1977. Att. 7,000. Result W 1-0. Scorer, Ian Wallace. *Mid-season away friendly. Played at Qali Stadium in Valletta.*

v Saudi Arabia February 6, 1978. Result L 0-4. *A depleted squad made the 17 hour return journey to Riyadh. The players who missed out were Oakey, Roberts, Holton, Graydon, Yorath and Nardiello.*

v Malta XI December 13, 1978. Result W 6-1. *Mid-season away friendly. Played at Qali Stadium in Valletta.*

v Faroe Islands May 9, 1979. Att. 4,000. Result W 6-0. Scorers: Ferguson (3), Wallace (2), Powell. *Match to celebrate Faeroe Islands' FA 75th. Anniversary. Played in Tórshavn.*

v New York Cosmos (USA) May 16, 1979. Att. 30,000. Result L 1-3. Scorer: Hunt. *Match staged as part of the deal that took Steve Hunt to Coventry from Cosmos. Venue was the Meadowlands Stadium, Rutherford, New Jersey. Fittingly, Coventry's goal was scored by returning hero Hunt. Pele played for Cosmos. It was the second time he faced City, having played for Santos in 1972 in a friendly in Bangkok.*

v Nicosia XI November 19, 1980. Att. 6,000. Result D 2-2. Scorers: Jacobs, Thompson. *Played in Cyprus. Mid-season away friendly.*

v Benfica July 31, 1983. Att. 30,000. Result D 2-2. Scorers: Butterworth, Bamber. *Played in Lisbon against the Portuguese Champions. Teenage goalie Tim Dalton played as Perry Suckling was unavailable.*

v. Gibraltar Select XI. May 19, 1986. Result W 3-1. Scorers: Culpin (2), Brazil. *Played in Gibraltar.*

v Los Boliches (Spain). September 10, 1987. Result W 2-0. Scorers: Gynn, Bennett. *Mid-season away friendly against Spanish Division 3 Champions. Played in Fuengirola.*

v Hong Kong XI May 14, 1988. Att. 15,000. Result W 2-1. Scorers: Speedie, Regis. *"Carlsberg Challenge Cup."*

v Boulevard (Bermuda) v Middlesbrough. February 28 and March 3, 1989. Result v Boulevard W 4-0. Scorers: Bannister, Bennett, Emerson, Regis. Result v Boro W 2-1. Scorers: Regis, Clark. *Knocked out of the FA Cup (to Sutton U.), Coventry fix up a mid-season, two team, short tour to Bermuda. Played in Hamilton. See also: Summer Tours.*

PENALTY SHOOT OUTS

Like England, the Sky Blues have an unhappy history in penalty shoot-outs, having lost three of the four they have taken part in.

Easily the most crucial – and disappointing – failure was in the the FA Cup Quarter Final replay against Sheffield United at Bramall Lane in March 1998.

Thanks to an early goal from Paul Telfer, City were seconds away from a first FA Cup semi-final appearance since 1987. But David Holdsworth's goal in the last minute of normal time, and a goalless period of extra time, ensured a penalty shoot-out. The tone was set for City when the hithertoo unerring Dion Dublin missed the first penalty. As it was, only Telfer of City's four penalty takers was successful and the Blades were gifted progression.

City's only success in a penalty shoot-out was against Peterborough United in the League Cup in 2001, Roland Nilsson's first game in charge.

v West Ham United (h) Winston Churchill Trophy. Mar. 3, 1967. Att. 18,524. Result 3-3. Scorers: Gibson, Machin (2).
Penalty Shoot-out: no details available
Lost 7-9

v Reading (a) Simod Cup Semi-Final. Mar. 2, 1988. Att. 15,348. Result (aet) 1-1. Scorer: Speedie.
Penalty Shoot-out: Kilcline (goal), Downs (goal), Sedgley (missed), Smith (goal), Bennett (missed).
Lost 3-4.

v Sheffield United (a) FA Cup R6 replay. Mar. 17, 1998. Result (aet) 1-1. Scorer: Telfer.
Penalty Shoot-out: Dublin (missed), Haworth (missed), Telfer (goal), Burrows (missed)
Lost 1-3.

v Peterborough United (a) League Cup R2. Sep. 11, 2001. Att. 5,729. Result D 2-2. Scorers: Carsley, Thompson.
Penalty Shoot-out: Thompson (goal), Bothroyd (goal), Hughes (goal), Hedman (missed), Carsley (goal)
Won 4-2.

PLACE IN THE SUN

The following players have gone to live or work abroad in non-football jobs:

Gordon Nutt Film Production, Australia
Arthur Lightening South Africa
Bill Glazier Swimming Pool maintenance in Costa Blanca, Spain
Dave Clements Irish goods shop in Georgetown, Colorado, USA
Larry Lloyd Property in Costa del Sol, Spain
Alan Miller Holidays in Majorca, Spain
David Burrows Dordogne in France

PLASTIC PITCHES

One of the few innovations that Coventry City did not pioneer was the synthetic pitch. This is because they were rubbish. Yet, given City's success on plastic, maybe the board should have taken the plunge.

Artificial grass was developed in the USA in the late 1960s to provide all-weather playing surfaces. Two types of synthetic pitch were originally created – Astroturf and Tartan. With an estimated cost in excess of £150,000 in 1969, the new surface was too expensive for most clubs and it took some years of further development before the plastic surface was suitable for football.

It was in 1981 that the first artificial playing surface in English football was introduced by Queens Park Rangers at Loftus Road. Their "Omniturf" surface was installed for a cost of £350,000.

The Sky Blues played five times against both QPR and Luton Town on their synthetic playing surfaces. Although the synthetic carpets were generally slammed by many visiting managers, Coventry won twice at each venue.
In the 1985-86 season City won at both QPR and at Luton, becoming the first side to beat Luton on their artificial pitch.

Coventry City never played at Oldham Athletic or Preston North End during the time that those clubs had plastic pitches.

PLAYER OF THE YEAR

Continued from Sky Blue Heaven Vol I
Voted by the fans:
2002-03	Mohammed Konjic
2003-04	Julian Joachim
2004-05	Stephen Hughes

Players' Player of the Year:
2002-03	Richard Shaw
2003-04	Calum Davenport
2004-05	Stephen Hughes

PRE-SEASON COMPETITIONS

Over the years, City have entered a number of "competitions" which were pre-season friendlies with the added spice of a third team to make it into a mini-tournament.

Sometimes they were even given a name to make them sound even more important. Who, after all, can forget the Skol Festival? Er, well, most of us, I suppose...

Anyway, here's a full list of these wondrous events. The memories will come flooding back!

1979 Hearts v Hibernian v Coventry City v Manchester City. Aug 4-8.
"Skol Festival." Pre-season four team tournament at Tynecastle and Easter Road grounds, Edinburgh. Coventry beat Manchester City 3-1 (English 2, Ferguson), then Hearts by the same scoreline (Hateley, Hunt, o.g.) and after a 0-0 with Hibernian, the Sky

Blues won the trophy.

1991 Kilmarnock v Rangers v Coventry City v Sparta Rotterdam (Netherlands). Aug 2-4.
Four team tournament at Rugby Park, Kilmarnock. It's a disastrous pre-season preparation in Scotland. Peake, Sansom and McGrath are sent home for breaking a curfew. Then City lose 1-3 at Ayr. In the mini-tournament they drew 1-1 with Rangers (Furlong) but lost on penalties. In the 3rd/4th place match, they lost 1-2 to Sparta (Billing). Rangers won the trophy.

1992 Birmingham City v Coventry City v Brescia (Italy) v Real Mallorca (Spain). Aug 8-9.
Pre-season four-team tournament at St. Andrews, Birmingham. The Sky Blues beat Brescia 1-0 (Smith) then lost 0-1 to Birmingham who thus became proud holders of the "Apex Asphalt International Trophy."

1995 Aberdeen v Coventry City Aug 12, Result W 5-1.
Scorers: Ndlovu (3), Dublin (2). *"Caledonian Trophy Match" at Pittodrie. Because of its fancy billing this pre-season friendly gets a mention. Future City player Eoin Jess scored for Aberdeen.*

2005 San Antonio (Spain) v Huddersfield v QPR v Coventry City, Jul 11-14.
This four-team tournament, called the Copa Ibiza and staged on the Balearic Island ended in some rancour after City lost 3-2 to QPR in the 'final' after being 2-0 up thanks to goals from Dele Adebola and Gary McSheffrey. Micky Adams' team reached the final thanks to a 1-0 win over Huddersfield Town (McSheffrey).

PUBS

Football and pubs seem to go together, so it is probably appropriate that so many ex-Sky Blues players went into the licensed trade after their playing days were over.

An early example was Nat Robinson (1895-1915), a retired goalkeeper who was landlord of the Red Horse public house near Highfield Road, when he made a playing comeback.

Nat had originally joined Singer's FC as a half-back, but played in goal in a reserve match as an emergency and found that goalkeeper was his best position.

He left soon after and had several seasons at Small Heath then Chelsea. By 1910, when Robinson re-joined the club he had started with, Singer's had become Coventry City. He played twice for City before retiring in 1911 to run the Red Horse.

During the 1914-15 war-time season, regular goalie Sid Blake was injured and 36-year-old Robinson was asked to step in. He conceded nine goals in a 1-9 defeat at Stoke and called time on his career once and for all after five appearances in 1915.

***

Public houses also played a prominent role in the early days of the club's history. Singer's Football Club was founded at the "Lord Aylesford Inn" Hillfields, in October 1883.

The first headquarters of the club was "The White Lion" in the Gosford Green area to the north of the City. In 1887, when the club moved to the Stoke Road ground, City's headquarters became the "Binley Oak" on Paynes Lane.

***

In October 1962, Coventry City opened The Sky Blue Club at Highfield Road. The bar was officially opened by cricketer Dennis Compton and the Lord Mayor and Lady Mayoress of Coventry were in attendance to drink a toast. The club was a place where the fans could "rub shoulders" with the players after the game.

The Binley Oak, pictured in 1896, proudly displaying its Coventry City connections

***

The tradition for pulling pints continued when the club opened its own pub in 1966. Named The Sky Blue, the inn at Coundon Green was launched with full ceremony by the Chairman Derrick Robins, Manager Jimmy Hill and the City playing squad.

The club announced to the fans that the pub was "just for you." The pub was available for wedding receptions and private parties.

Business lunches cost from 5 shillings and sixpence and chicken in the basket was available in all bars. Some time later the public house was sold and reverted to its original name, "The Nugget."

***

The club also owned the Sky Blue Tavern opposite Highfield Road for several years. Standing on the corner of Swan Lane and Thackhall Street, it was formerly The Mercer's Arms, named after the company that used to own the land which both the pub and Highfield Road stood on.

The former City player and coach Brian Roberts met his future wife Alice at the Mercers. Her family ran the pub during the 1970s. Sadly City didn't display the same inn-keeping skills as the Brolly family. (Alice's brother is Bob Brolly of BBC CWR Radio) and the pub was demolished in 2002.

***

Some of the Coventry City publicans:
Nat Robinson Red Horse, Coventry
Billy Yates Dyers Arms, Coventry
George Chaplin Pub in Marton, Warwickshire
Frank Herbert Pub in Bedworth
Jack Snape Old Crown, Bedworth
George Mason New Star in Tile Hill, Coventry
Roy Kirk Royal Oak, Peterborough
Bob Wesson Royal Oak, Kenilworth

GOAL IN SIXTY SECONDS
Coventry City's Quickest Strikes

Mick Ferguson

7 seconds Ken Hale v Bristol Rovers (a) Apr 4 1964 W 1-0
14 seconds Mark Hateley v Southampton (a) Jan 15 1983 D 1-1
14 seconds Youssef Chippo v Barnsley (h) Feb 23 2002 W 4-0
25 seconds Mick Ferguson v Birmingham City (h) Mar 4 1978 W 4-0
27 seconds Gerry Daly v Stoke City (h) Nov 24 1981 W 3-0
28 seconds Steve Livingstone v Chelsea (h) Feb 3 1990 W 3-2
35 seconds Gerry Daly v Liverpool (h) Sep 22 1981 L 1-2
39 seconds Gary McAllister v Bradford City (a) Nov 6 1999 D 1-1
42 seconds Dave Bennett v Newcastle United (a) Jan 3 1987 W 2-1
45 seconds Nicky Platnauer v Liverpool (h) Dec 10 1983 W 4-0
45 seconds Paul Telfer v Crystal Palace (a) Feb 28 1998 W 3-0
49 seconds Craig Bellamy v Leicester City (a) Apr 7 2001 W 3-1
53 seconds Peter Barnes v West Bromwich Albion (h) Nov 24 1984 L 2-5
56 seconds Lee Dixon (og) v Arsenal (a) Sep 7 1991 W 2-1
57 seconds Mick Ferguson v Leicester City (h) Oct 2 1976 D 1-1
59 seconds Mick Ferguson v Liverpool (a) Sep 4 1976 L 1-3
First minute Ron Newman v Southampton(h) Mar 17 1956 W 2-0*
First minute Steve Hunt v Sunderland (h) Oct 21 1980 W 2-1*
*No exact time recorded

John Tudor Pub in Derbyshire
Ernie Hunt Full Pitcher, Ledbury
Noel Cantwell New Inn, Peterborough
Larry Lloyd Pub in Nottingham
Jim Holton Rising Sun & Old Stag, Coventry
Jim Blyth Pub in Nuneaton

Coventry City Hoteliers:
Charlie Elliott Nottingham
Gary Bannister St. Ives, Cornwall
Paul Edwards Coventry
Terry Butcher Bridge Of Allan, Scotland

QUICKEST GOALS

It always pays to arrive at the match nice and early. Not only do you avoid annoying your fellow-supporters, but you make sure that you are not caught out, missing an early goal. As this list proves, they do happen! It is worth noting that City have only ever lost three times after scoring in the first minute.

● Mick Ferguson was City's undisputed king of the lightning strike. The Sky Blues striker perfomed the feat three times – two of them in the space of six weeks in the autumn of 1976. Gerry Daly also perfomed the feat twice in one season, in 1981.

● Ron Newman is the only City player to score within a minute of his debut. Newman scored at Highfield Road against Southampton in March 1996. No exact time of the goal is recorded.

● Hugh Barr scored just 30 seconds after Coventry City kicked off in their first ever match in Sky Blue colours, a friendly game. *See: Various Odds and Ends.*

QUOTES

Here's a selection of quotes from players and managers who opened their mouths and put their foot in them – as only footballers can.

"England have three fresh men with three fresh legs." *Jimmy Hill.*

"Beckham has two feet which a lot of players don't have nowadays." *Jimmy Hill.*

"There's a rat in the camp throwing a spanner in the works." *Chris Cattlin*

"We didn't come here tonight to get any sort of result." *Les Sealey*

"I can see the carrot at the end of the tunnel." *Stuart Pearce*

"Give him his head and he'll take it with both hands and feet." *Bobby Gould*

"It's thrown a spanner in the fire." *Bobby Gould*

"He held his head in his hands as it flashed past the post." *Alan Brazil*

"The only way forwards is backwards." *Dave Sexton*

"Venison and Butcher – they're as brave as two peas in a pod." *John Sillett*

"There are nil-nils and nil-nils and this was nil-nil." *John Sillett*

"It's a case of putting all your eggs into 90 minutes." *Phil Neal*

"The ball came over mine and Calderwood's heads and who should be there at the far post – yours truly Alan Shearer." *Colin Hendry*

"Now the world is my lobster." *Keith O'Neill*

"I can't even remember when the 70s was." *Robbie Keane*

"I think that the replay showed it to be worse than it actually was." *Ron Atkinson*

"Beckenbauer has gambled all his eggs." *Ron Atkinson*

"I think it was a moment of cool panic there." *Ron Atkinson*

"It's all about the two Ms - movement and positioning." *Ron Atkinson*

"They must go for it now as they have nothing to lose but the match." *Ron Atkinson*

"They've picked their heads up off the ground and now they have a lot to carry on their shoulders." *Ron Atkinson*

"Either side could win it or it could be a draw." *Ron Atkinson*

"Zero - zero is a big score." *Ron Atkinson*

"He sliced the ball when he had it on a plate." *Ron Atkinson.*

RECORD RECEIPTS

HIGHFIELD ROAD
£405,369.   v. Charlton Athletic. FA Cup R.5.
January 29, 2000.

NEUTRAL
£1,286,737. v. Tottenham Hotspur. FA Cup Final.
May 16, 1987. Wembley.

Ronnie Rees (centre) looks on as his Sky Blues team-mates celebrate a goal

REES, RONNIE

A major player in the Sky Blue era of the 1960s, Ronnie Rees is fondly remembered by those who saw him play.

Starting with the Coventry City youth side, Rees turned professional in April 1962 and graduated to the first team in September of the same year. Once manager Jimmy Hill had given him his debut, in a home game against Shrewsbury Town, there was no turning back. The Welshman was an integral part of the 1964 Division Three Championship team, making 46 appearances and scoring 13 goals. His play on either wing was also a feature of the 1967 Division Two Championship side.

In his six years at Highfield Road, Ronnie was an automatic choice for Coventry. His tireless running and wing play set up many goals for his team mates. He also scored plenty for himself and ranks inside the top 20 all-time goalscorers for City.

Quick as lightning, Rees' dazzling displays excited the fans while opposition defences struggled to contain him. Ronnie's talents led, not surprisingly, to international caps for Wales. He made 21 appearances for the Welsh national side as a City man.

In 1968, manager Noel Cantwell balanced the club's books with a £65,000 deal that saw Rees move to local rivals, West Bromwich Albion. Although Ronnie had amassed more than 260 appearances for the Sky Blues by then, he was still only 24-years-old.

After a season at Albion he moved on and continued playing in Division One in the Midlands, with Nottingham Forest.

While at the City Ground Ronnie suffered one of the harshest ever punishments in English football history, when he was given six weeks' suspension on January 22, 1970.

His crime was to be cautioned three times that season. His bookings in games against Leeds, Everton and Arsenal were considered by an FA Commission in Birmingham to be worthy of the lengthy ban. He was also fined £100.

Ronnie Rees finished his career at Swansea City, and by the time he hung up his boots he had won 39 caps for Wales, scoring three goals.

After retiring from football, Ronnie worked for the Ford motor company at Bridgend but after suffering a stroke in 1995, is now retired and lives in Swansea. His eldest son played football for both Cardiff City and Swansea City.
1962-68. 262 apps. 52 goals.

REID, PETER

Peter Reid was a highly respected midfield player with Everton, Bolton Wanderers and England. He managed Manchester City, Sunderland and Leeds United, with diminishing success. After leaving Leeds United he became a regular pundit on BBC Television live football coverage.

He returned to the game when he was appointed Coventry City manager in May 2004 following the unexpected sacking of Eric Black. He was arguably the least popular and least successful manager of Coventry City in living memory. Reid was in charge at Coventry City eight months, during which time a promising and attractive side became relegation candidates.

The team won one out of the last eight games in which he was in charge in the Coca-Cola Championship. Peter Reid left by mutual consent on January 6, 2005. He returned to his role as a BBC football expert.
Manager: May 2004–January 2005.
Managerial Stats: P31 W10 D8 L13 32.2% wins

RELATIVES

Three members of the Dennison family have Coventry City connections. Jack Dennison played three games for Coventry in 1922 and was the older brother of Bob Dennison, Chief Scout 1967-78. Richard Dennison, son of Bob, was assistant club secretary in the 1970s.

***

Brothers Jimmy and Archie Knox had a brief association with Coventry City. Jimmy played just two games for City, in the 1957-58 season. He went on to manage VS Rugby. His brother Archie became City first team coach in January 2004, replacing Gary Mills. The vastly experienced 57-

year-old was the former manager of Forfar and Dundee, assistant manager to Alex Ferguson at both Aberdeen and Manchester United and assistant to Walter Smith at both Rangers and Everton. He had also been assistant manager to Scotland. He was sacked on May 1st 2004.

***

The son of John Sillett (1962-66. 128 apps. 2 goals. Coach/Manager 1987-90), had a trial with Coventry City. Neil Sillett didn't make it as a player and became a physiotherapist. He was assistant to George Dalton at City in 1988 and later became club physio at Derby County.

Three generations of the Sillett family have been in football. John's father Charles played for Southampton, John and his brother Peter were team mates at Chelsea. Peter played three times for England in 1955.

***

Robert Betts (2000-03. 17 apps. 1 goal) is the grandson of Maurice Setters (1967-70. 59 apps. 3 goals). Setters was manager of Doncaster Rovers and assistant manager to Jack Charlton of the Ireland national side. In just two years after leaving Coventry City, Betts played for Rochdale, Kidderminster, Hereford, Forest Green Rovers and Racing Warwick.

***

Craig Pead (2002-05. 45 apps. 2 goals) is son of George Pead, Academy Operations Manager for the club. In the summer of 2005 he joined Walsall having played there on loan in 2004-05.

***

Ray Gooding (1976-82. 55 apps. 5 goals) and for many years the club's Football Development Officer, is father of reserve team player and England Youth cap, Andy Gooding.

REST IN PEACE
See page 84

ROBERTS, BRIAN

Brian was a rugged no-nonsense defender for nine seasons with the Sky Blues and having worked on the coaching side for many years, is one of the longest serving men in the club's history. A true character and affectionately known as "Harry" – although he is believed to be the only player to have been nicknamed after a notorious gangster and police murderer.

A one-club man – he has only ever played for one club at a time – he was born in Manchester and was spotted playing in midfield for Mercer Celtic and Manchester Boys by the father of former Coventry player Graham Paddon. He became a City apprentice in 1971 and, after a brief loan spell at Hereford United, turned professional in May 1975. He made his debut in April 1976 in a 4-1 defeat at Tottenham Hotspur.

Manager Gordon Milne did his best to keep Roberts away from critics and supporters. The first ten games that Roberts played for the club were away matches. Eventually, though, he had to play him in a game at Highfield Road, a 1-1 draw in April 1977 against Tottenham Hotspur.

Brian was used as emergency cover in a variety of defensive positions. After just 18 appearances, he had worn six different shirt numbers. During the 1977-78 season, Roberts got his chance to establish himself. Following Graham Oakey's injury at Villa Park over Christmas, he slotted into the right back role. It was surely no coincidence that this was to be the Sky Blues best season for years. Coventry finished a whisker away from Europe in 7th position.

Over the next two seasons, Brian saw less action as Mick Coop made a return to the side, but he made a full return in the 1980-81 season. After just one appearance, left-back Bobby McDonald was transferred to Manchester City and Milne switched Roberts to the vacated position. He played every game through to the end of the season and the side of young players reached the semi-finals of the League Cup.

City's new manager in 1981, Dave Sexton, juggled things a bit, but he too found that Roberts was the best man for the left-back role. In 1982-83 after 192 games Roberts surprised everyone, not least himself, by scoring two goals for the team.

The first one came in a 3-0 win at West Ham, the second in a FA Cup tie against Norwich. Evidently the tactic of lulling the opposition into complacency worked a treat. Unfortunately, Roberts had been rumbled and he never scored again. "I saw Harry Score" T-shirts and badges were produced to commemorate the event.

As the team's season deteriorated and became a desperate relegation struggle, Brian's 200th appearance landmark passed unrecognised in a 1-1 home draw against Tottenham in March.
In the summer of 1983, Bobby Gould replaced the sacked Dave Sexton as manager.

There were more comings and goings at the club than at Piccadilly Station but Brian Roberts stayed on. With Stuart Pearce on the left side of defence, Brian, ever honest and hardworking, made a return to the right-back position.

Having selected him for 30 appearances that 1983-84 season and made him captain, the maverick Gould declared that Roberts did not fit

Brian Roberts

into his plans and he was sold on transfer deadline day in March 1984 to Birmingham City for £10,000. Also out was Steve Hunt, as the club cashed in on their most valuable assets. £10,000 was obviously a lot of money in those days. Curiously, BBC Grandstand's "Football Focus" had just featured both players in an item about life as a player with Coventry City.

REST IN PEACE

The following former Coventry City chairmen, managers or players passed away between 1999 and 2005:

Erle Shanks d March 1999 (Chairman 1954-58)
Emilo Aldecoa d September 1999 (Player 1946-47 29 apps 2 goals)
Jack Fairbrother d October 1999 (Manager 1953-54)
John Burckitt d November 1999 (Player 1964-65 7 apps)
Jack Snape d February 2000 (Player 1937-50 111 apps 2 goals)
George Kirby d March 2000 (Player 1963-64 18 apps 10 goals)
Ken Keyworth d November 7 2000 (Player 1964-65 7 apps 3 goals)
Ray Straw d Ilkeston May 2001 (Player 1957-61 151 apps 85 goals)
Les Sealey d August 19 2001 (Player 1976-83 & 1991-92 180 apps)
Ron Hewitt d September 2001 (Player 1959-62 63 apps 24 goals)
Stewart Imlach d Formby October 2001 (Player 1960-62 79 apps 11 goals)
Arthur Lightening d Durban South Africa October 2001 (Player 1958-62 160 apps)
Reg Matthews d Coventry October 7 2001 (Player 1952-57 116 apps)
Alf Wood d Aberdare December 17 2001 (Player 1937-51 246 apps)
Roy Dwight d Woolwich April 9 2002 (Player 1961-63 33 apps 8 goals)
Pat Saward d Newmarket September 20 2002 (Coach Assistant Manager 1963-70)
Jim Sanders d August 14 2003 (Player 1958-59 10 apps)
Charlie Elliott MBE d Nottingham January 1 2004

Noel Cantwell welcomes Colin Randall with Bob Dennison (centre)

(Player 1931-48 101 apps 2 goals Caretaker-manager 1954-55)
Fred Bett d Scunthorpe April 14 2004 (Player 1946-48 27 apps 11 goals)
Derrick Robins d Cape Town South Africa May 3 2004 (Chairman 1960-73)
Frank Austin d Long Eaton July 13 2004 (Player 1952-63 313 apps 2 goals)
Jim Harrison d October 2004 (Player 1951-53 23 apps 3 goals)
Noel Cantwell d Peterborough September 8 2005 (Manager 1967-72)

Brian was briefly back at Highfield Road for his testimonial in September 1984, the first for a Coventry City player since Mick Coop's benefit seven years earlier. A "City Past" against "City Present" match ended in a 4-4 draw. Roberts spent six years at St Andrew's and became a "Blues Legend," making over 200 appearances between 1984 and 1990.

He moved on to Wolverhampton Wanderers and during his two years at Molyneux, Brian wrote a book on his footballing life, "Harry's Game." One of the most entertaining books written by any footballer, it's an insight into life at Coventry City and Birmingham City in the 1970s and 1980s and is a must for fans who were around at that time (or indeed weren't).

In 1992 Roberts returned to Coventry City to join the coaching staff as reserve team coach. During 1996 he moved from the reserves to become Youth Development Manager following the death of recruitment officer Bert Edwards. Among the young players under Brian's wing were Chris Kirkland, Gavin Strachan, Barry Quinn, John Eustace, Gary McSheffrey and Craig Pead. His column in the programme about the Youth side was always an entertaining read.

Don't mention sprouts to Brian. In March 1997, he took part in a "sproutathon," at a pub in Stretton-on-Dunsmore. Brian ate 120 sprouts in one hour and along with two friends raised £1,000 for Comic Relief.

Brian summed up the experience: "Never again! I ate the first 70 with gravy but then I started to feel sick and I don't know how I got through the rest. It has put me off sprouts for life."
At the end of the 1997-98 season, Roberts left the club. During his two spells combined, from becoming an apprentice as a sixteen-year-old in

1971, he had been with Coventry City for some 19 years.

Nowadays Brian is Head of Sport at a school in Leamington Spa where Rugby and Cricket are the main games. He remains loyal to the club and is a regular guest and match summariser on BBC Coventry & Warwickshire radio.
Player: 1976-84. 249 apps. 2 goals.
Coaching staff: 1992-98.

ROBINS, DERRICK
Derrick Robins was Coventry City's man of destiny. He was the man who more than any other, shaped the future of Coventry City.

Born on June 27, 1915 in Bexleyheath Kent, Derrick Harold Robins was a stockbroker's son. He first came to Coventry in 1937 and at one time sold cakes for a living. During the war he served in Egypt, Iraq, Persia, Palestine, India and Burma, climbing from Private to Major in the British Army.

In 1950 he founded the Banbury Buildings company and the success of the business turned Robins into a millionaire. Robins joined the board of Coventry City on April 25, 1954.

He served a six year apprenticeship before his appointment as chairman on October 17, 1960. This involved a switch with Walter Brandish junior who stepped down, becoming vice-chairman.

The worrying financial state of the club which Robins inherited was just the sort of challenge he relished. He was also fully aware of the old-fashioned, interfering style of chairmanship the club had experienced in the past. It had not exactly brought the club any success.

When Robins took over as chairman the club were a modest Division Three side, playing the likes of

Newport County, Torquay United, and Shrewsbury Town and they had won only four games out of 16 that 1960-61 season. By the time he handed over to his successor in 1973, Coventry City were an established Division One team having played in Europe.

Robins set about transforming the club, formulating a new board. Next he turned to the Highfield Road ground. "It had a terrible entrance to it and the whole place seemed to cry out: 'Don't come in.' I felt we needed a smart entrance to make people feel welcome, plus a decent manager's office and boardroom.The problem was that we had no money. So I told the other directors 'You put in what you can afford and I'll make up the rest.' From then on we were pulling together. "I also said that no director must charge a farthing to the club."

Fortunately for City, Robins had more than just money to offer. He had foresight and ambition, with an uncanny knack for taking a gamble and winning. It was a couple of cup defeats that were the prelude to Robins bringing in a new manager. A 3-0 stuffing in the League Cup at Workington in September 1961 was, by all accounts, the worst performance by a Coventry City team anyone could remember. By the time City were getting knocked out of the FA Cup by non-league Kings Lynn 2-1 at home two months later, Robins knew who would be the new boss.

Indeed, he was watching in the stand that day, trying to keep his distinctive chin tucked inside the collar of his overcoat. Jimmy Hill was appointed a few days later and a new partnership was born. Robins gave Hill a free reign to run team matters his own way. The official statement referred to the new manager being given "complete control." The board's job was to organise the finances of the club. Robins made a personal contribution to that effect, by making a £30,000 gift to the club. Hill could go into the transfer market.

It was enough money to buy five new players. That was just the start and the flow of players in and out of the club continued. At the same time changes off the field were equally impressive. The Sky Blue era, as it became known, was an exciting period of innovation. Robins was not hindered by convention or tradition. He found new ways of bringing revenue to the club such as the Sky Blue Pool which emerged from the small beginnings of the Bantams Fighting Fund. The money that now came in meant that if Hill sold players it was for football reasons, rather than to appease the bank manager.

Robins was a dynamic and decisive supporter of Jimmy Hill's plans. One day in 1962 is a good example. The two men flew to Ireland and signed Willy Humphries and Hugh Barr from Ards and Linfield respectively. On the way back in the plane to London, Hill mentioned that he was interested in another player, John Sillett of Chelsea. Robins reply was that they should go straight to Stamford Bridge from the airport.

They did a quick deal with Tommy Docherty and persuaded the player that the move was in his interests. They even convinced John's wife before returning to Coventry.

Robins went along with every one of Hill's plans, innovations and schemes and had plenty of ideas of his own. In the mid-1960s he had envisaged a time when football clubs would have a range of facilities. He foresaw a Highfield Road with a bowling alley, restaurants, a garage, a dance hall, a social centre, squash courts and facilities to make it the hub of the city's sporting facilities.

Doing The Business: Derrick Robins (centre, seated)

Robins' favourite phrase was: "People matter."

On the field, Coventry City enjoyed the success of two Championship titles in 1964 and 1967. Only after the club had achieved First Division status in 1967, did the partnership of almost six years came to an end.

Hill had wanted a 10 year contract, while Robins had offered him half that and the two proud men failed to find a compromise. Hill was succeeded by Noel Cantwell.

Having achieved so much together, Robins and

Hill went their separate ways without acrimony. As the team became established in the top division Robins saw that Highfield Road was transformed into a modern stadium. International matches and Inter-League games were staged. Derrick Robins continued as chairman of the club until, having suffered several heart attacks, he stepped down in May 1973. He had been chairman for 13 remarkable years.

Derrick Robins became Life President of the club and was succeeded as chairman briefly by his son Peter and then by Sir Jack Scamp. Robins left

Britain in April 1975 for tax reasons and went to live in South Africa.

In September 1995, chairman Bryan Richardson and the board revoked the position of Life President that had been bestowed on Robins. Robins, clearly offended, responded that the honour was "for as long as I live. My heart and soul is with the Sky Blues and always will be."
Derrick Robins passed away in Cape Town in May 2004 at the age of 90.
Chairman 1960-73.
See: Cricketers.

SCORED ON DEBUT

Here is a list of all the players who have scored on their debut for Coventry City FC:

George Hadley v Rotherham Cnty Aug 28 1920 W 3-2
Sam Foster v Cardiff City Dec 25 1920 L 2-4
Albert Howell v Wolverhampton W Feb 24 1921 W 4-0
Thomas Wolfe v Barnsley Aug 25 1923 L 2-3
Herbert Pearson v Hull City Dec 6 1924 L 1-4
Albert Pynegar v Port Vale Jan 26 1924 D 1-1
William Paterson v Lincoln City Aug 29 1926 W 3-2
William Stoddart v Watford Aug 27 1927 D 1-1
Peter Ramage v Swindon Town Sep 5 1927 W 4-0
Randolph Galloway v Torquay Utd Jan 14 1928 W 5-1
Danny Shone v Brighton & HA Jan 5 1929 W 3-0
Frank Bowden v Clapton Orient Oct 5 1929 W 5-2
Tommy Bowen (2 goals) v Norwich Aug 25 1928 W 3-0
John Starsmore v Brentford Oct 6 1928 W 1-0
John Phillips v Clapton Orient Sep 6 1930 D 3-3
Jack Cull v Fulham Aug 29 1931 L 3-5
Jock Lauderdale v Fulham Aug 29 1931 L 3-5
Harry Holmes v Crystal Palace Feb 6 1932 W 8-0
Billy Frith v Newport County Sep 17 1932 W 3-1
Reuben Woolhouse v Crystal P Nov 5 1932 W 3-1
George Blytheway v Charlton Ath Oct 14 1933 W 3-2
Robert Birtley v Northampton T Aug 25 1934 W 2-0

Charlie Wilson v Crystal P Oct 13 1934 L 1-3
Tommy Crawley v Cardiff City Feb 22 1936 W 5-1
Ellis Lager v Bournemouth Apr 18 1936 W 2-0
Ted Roberts v Burnley Mar 26 1937 D 3-3
George Taylor v Luton Town Oct 9 1937 W 2-1
Lol Coen v West Ham United Sep17 1938 L 1-4
Fred Bett v Burnley Aug 31 1946 D 1-1
Iain Jamieson v Leeds United Jan 15 1949 W 4-1
Jack Evans v Fulham Apr 2 1949 W 1-0
Tommy Briggs v Bury Dec 30 1950 W 5-2
Gordon Nutt v Blackburn Rovers Dec 29 1951 L 1-2
Charlie Dutton v Bournemouth Sep 14 1953 W 2-0
Jackie Lee (2 goals) v Crystal P Nov 27 1954 W 4-1
Alan Moore v Southampton Dec 25 1954 D 1-1
Ken McPherson v Newport County Dec 10 1955 W 3-0
Ron Newman v Southampton Mar 17 1956 W 2-0*
Dennis Churms v Exeter City Aug 18 1956 W 1-0
Jack Boxley v Southend United Dec 29 1956 W 2-1
Brian Hill v Gillingham Apr30 1958 L 2-3
George Stewart v Chester Nov 29 1958 W 5-1
Terry Bly v Notts County Aug 18 1962 W 2-0
Hugh Barr v Notts County Aug 18 1962 W 2-0
George Hudson (3 goals) v Halifax T Apr 6 1963 W 5-4
Ken Keyworth v Rotherham Utd Dec 51964 L 3-5
Dave Clements v Northampton T Jan 23 1965 D 1-1
Ray Pointer v Norwich City Dec 27 1965 D 1-1
Les Cartwright (sub) v Leicester C Sep 29 1973 W 2-0
Steve Hunt v Derby County Sep 2 1978 W 2-0
Martin Singleton v Everton Apr 13 1982 W 1-0
Terry Gibson v Watford Aug 27 1983 L 2-3
Graham Withey (sub) v Tottenham Aug 29 1983 D 1-1
Paul Culpin (sub) v Oxford Utd Sep 3 1985 W 5-2
Alan Brazil v Newcastle United Feb 1 1986 L 2-3
David Speedie v Tottenham Aug 15 1987 W 2-1
Kevin Drinkell v Grimsby T Oct 4 1989 (L Cup) W 3-0
Sean Flynn v Sheffield Utd Dec26 1991 W 3-0
John Williams v Middlesbrough Aug 15 1992 W 2-1
Mick Quinn (2 goals) v Manchester C Nov 21 1992 L 2-3
Mick Harford (sub) v Newcastle Utd Aug 18 1993 W 2-1
Dion Dublin v Queens Park Rangers Sep 10 1994 D 2-2
Graham Barratt v Peterborough Utd Aug 13 2003 League Cup R1 W 2-0
Dele Adebola v Peterborough Utd Aug 13 2003 League Cup R1 W 2-0

David Speedie

Johnnie Jackson (sub) v Crystal P Nov 29 2003 D 1-1
(on loan from Tottenham H)
Eddie Johnson v Sunderland Aug 7 2004 W 2-0
(on loan from Manchester United)
Stern John v Gillingham (pen) Sep 15 2004 D 2-2
Players listed chronologically 1919 onwards
*See: Quickest Goals

SCOTLAND INTERNATIONALS

The following Coventry City players represented
Scotland. Caps while playing with Coventry - first
figure. (Total number of caps in brackets.)

Willie Carr	6 (6)	1970-72
Colin Stein	4 (21)	1973
Tommy Hutchison	17 (17)	1973-75
Jim Blyth	2 (2)	1978
Ian Wallace	3 (3)	1978-79
David Speedie	5 (10)	1988-89
Kevin Gallacher	10 (53)	1990-93
Eoin Jess	3 (17)	1996-97
Gary McAllister	13 (57)	1996-99
Paul Telfer	1 (1)	2000
Colin Hendry	5 (51)	2000

Also Represented Scotland:
Gordon Strachan 50 caps - *Aberdeen, Manchester United, Leeds United 1980-92.* (City player & Manager 1995-2001)
Eric Black 2 caps - *Metz 1988.* (City Assistant Manager 2002-04. Manager 2004)

SENT OFF

Coventry City's worst ever season for red cards was the season after relegation 2001-02 with ten sendings off. Three of them went to **David Thompson** who became the first City player to be sent off three times in one campaign.

Paul Williams, better known as Willo, who played for the Sky Blues between 1995 and 2001, was the only Coventry City player ever to be sent off four times, twice away and twice at Highfield Road. Perhaps the most famous time was in January 1998 at home to Arsenal when non-flying Dutchman Dennis Bergkamp performed a dying swan worthy of Sadlers Wells ballet. City put in a stalwart performance to hold the team that went on to be champions to a 2-2 draw, and perhaps deseved victory.

In April 1975 **Chris Cattlin** became the first ever Coventry City player to be dismissed twice, getting his marching orders at Upton Park against West Ham, having previously got the first use of the bath almost four years earlier against Everton at Goodison Park in October 1971. Amazingly, City won both games.

As it is though, statistical analysis reveals that City are almost three times as likely to lose an away game with ten men as win it, whereas at home, City have won just as many as lost with a man short.

While playing for Birmingham City, **Liam Daish** was sent off in a game against Chester. A fan had thrown a trumpet onto the pitch and Daish picked it up and started playing it. The humourless referee dismissed him for ungentlemanly conduct.

Patrick Suffo has a habit of seeing red. Playing for Cameroon in the Japan 2002 World Cup finals against Germany, he came on as a 53rd minute substitute. He collected two yellow cards in 23 minutes and was dismissed. A total of 16 yellow and two red cards were shown in the game – a record.

Suffo was also sent off while playing for Sheffield United in March 2002, along with two team mates. The match against West Bromwich Albion was abandoned when three injuries reduced the Blades to six men on the field.

Carlton Palmer has the unique record of being sent off while playing for each of his five Premiership clubs: Sheffield Wednesday, Leeds United, Southampton, Nottingham Forest, Coventry City.
For a full list of Coventry City players sent off in League and Cup games, see Appendix.

SEXTON, DAVE OBE

The son of middleweight boxer Archie Sexton, Dave played for Chelmsford City, Luton Town, West Ham United, Leyton Orient, Brighton & H.A. and Crystal Palace. An inside forward, he had a good spell at Brighton, scoring 69 goals in 163 games helping them to the Championship of Division Three(S) in 1958.

Sexton retired from playing following a knee injury and joined the coaching staff at Chelsea. He took his first managerial job at Leyton Orient in 1965. After a spell coaching at Arsenal, he became manager of Chelsea in October 1967.

He enjoyed a successful time at Stamford Bridge, winning the FA Cup in 1970 and the European Cup Winners Cup a year later, when Chelsea beat Real Madrid 2-1 in a replayed final. Sexton began a little superstition at this time, carrying a rabbit's foot in his suit pocket as a lucky charm.

Dave Sexton

In October 1974 he was sacked by Chelsea after a poor start to the season and moved a few weeks later the short distance in West London to Queens Park Rangers. He took them to within a point of winning the League Championship in 1976, when they were runners-up to Liverpool.

Sexton resigned from the QPR job in 1977 and moved to Manchester United. During his time at Old Trafford, they reached the FA Cup final in 1979 and finished runners-up in the league in 1980. However, the Manchester United board expected more trophies and wanted a more extrovert style. He was sacked in 1981, replaced with his managerial opposite in flamboyant Ron Atkinson.

Coventry City engaged Dave Sexton in the summer of 1981 to succeed Gordon Milne. By now he was a vastly experienced coach and he had a number of promising youngsters to work with: Danny Thomas, Brian Roberts, Gary Gillespie, Steve Whitton and Garry Thompson were among them. However, Sexton didn't have strength in depth and his time at Highfield Road was to prove a difficult experience.

Sexton's first season in charge, 1981-82, was one of contrasts. An opening day win over his old club Manchester United 2-1, was also City's first ever three points for a victory. Then a bad run in the autumn was followed by a decent one and City finished just below mid-table in 14th position. It was no coincidence that the improved form followed the signing of Gerry Francis from QPR in January 1982, as his performances were of the highest quality.

Two stand-out matches were a 6-1 thrashing of Sunderland and a 5-5 draw at Southampton. Striker Mark Hateley scored five goals in the two games and Whitton copied the achievement with a hat-trick in a 3-1 win at Manchester City.

As managers go, Dave Sexton was not a natural wheeler-dealer. It was just as well as he had few wheels on his wagon to trade with, in a cash-strapped era for Coventry. The 1982-83 season started reasonably well and by February 1983, following a really good run and a 4-0 thrashing of Manchester City, the Sky Blues were in the top five. Having taken his previous three clubs – Chelsea, QPR & Manchester United into Europe – Sexton was looking to do the same with the Sky Blues. If only the season could have ended there

and then. His lucky rabbit's foot would fail him this time.

Sexton was disagreed with the club's shock decision to sell striker Garry Thompson to West Bromwich for a £225,000 fee. With the departure of Gerry Daly, who did not fit into Sexton's plans, it left him with just 14 senior players. Those who remained capitulated in the very next game. The 1-5 defeat in February at Notts County was as bad as it sounds. It began a run of 13 games without a win.

The team plummeted towards the drop zone. Behind the scenes there were wranglings over players' contracts.

Perhaps they were demoralised, but the performances by some of the players showed, to coin a modern phrase, that they were not fit to wear the shirt. This was demonstrated by one impassioned supporter. Having seen enough during a 0-1 home defeat to Birmingham, the fan ran onto the pitch and threw his Sky Blue jersey onto the field in disgust.

City finished 1982-83 one point and one place clear of relegation and Dave Sexton was sacked on the last day of the season. He would never manage a league team again.

In 1984 Sexton was appointed as the first Technical Director of the FA National School at Lilleshall. Whilst he was manager of the England U-21s, the national side won the UEFA U-21 Nations Cup twice.

Sexton became part of the England coaching staff under Sven-Goran Eriksson. Although he kept himself in the background, he had a significant role. He left the position on August 13, 2004, but continued with the England set-up in a scouting capacity. He was awarded the OBE on June 10, 2005.

Manager: May 1981 – May 1983.
Managerial Statistics: P96 W30 D24 L42 31.2% wins

SHAW, RICHARD

Ron Atkinson went on a spending spree when he took over as manager in February 1995 and one of the players he brought in was central defender Richard Shaw from Crystal Palace for a £1m. fee in November 1995. It has proved to be one of his best pieces of business.

Richard Shaw was born in Brentford on September 11, 1968. He played for Surrey Schoolboys and became an apprentice at Crystal Palace, making his debut for the south London side in 1986. In December 1989 he played four games on loan at Hull City, but returned to become a fixture in the Palace line-up. The highlight was playing in the 1990 FA Cup Final against Manchester United, which went to a replay before Palace were beaten. Richard was in the Palace side that won 4-1 at Highfield Road in November 1994 and also played when City gained revenge, winning at Selhurst Park the same season.

That match would be Phil Neal's last game in charge, signalling the start of "Big Ron's" reign. In total, Shaw made 207 appearance for Crystal Palace scoring three goals.

One other moment of incident in Richard's Palace career has gone down in history as the "Cantona Kung Fu Kick" affair in January 1995. Everyone who saw the television pictures remembers the moment when Manchester United's Cantona launched himself into the crowd and kicked, Kung Fu-style, at a man in the crowd who he claimed

Richard Shaw

was racially abusing him. Less well remembered is what led to the incident. A succession of tough tackles by Palace players resulted in Cantona totally losing his rag.

The Frenchman finally retaliated to a Richard Shaw tackle and was sent off by the referee. The red card enraged him further and over ten years on, the incident is still a vivid memory to those who saw it.

After signing for the Sky Blues, Shaw made his debut in a 1-1 draw at Queens Park Rangers. He had been relegated with his previous club and was immediately in another battle against the drop with Coventry. In only his third appearance he was sent off, receiving two yellow cards in a 3-3 home draw with Wimbledon.

Richard struck up a good partnership with Paul 'Willo' Williams in the centre of defence and was an automatic choice during Gordon Strachan's managerial tenure. With well-timed tackles, heading ability and speed, he was reliable and cool under pressure.

He even managed to niggle Manchester United boss Alex Ferguson who, in his autobiography, accused Shaw of being a shirt-puller. However, Richard's outstanding performances were recognised by the Coventry fans when he was voted Player of the Year for 1998-99.
Displaying a loyalty to the club that is almost unheard of in modern football, Shaw has been unfortunate to be playing for struggling sides. When City were relegated in 2001, many players left over the following year or so, but Shaw stayed on.

Shaw has always been the last line of defence for the Sky Blues. This gave him no chance to get forward and it seemed he was destined to go through his entire Coventry career without scoring a goal. To everyone's great surprise and delight, Shaw avoided that with a screamer of a shot against Gillingham on May 1st, 2004, in a 5-2 away win

Richard Shaw passed a significant landmark against Sunderland on August 7, 2004, when he made his 300th. appearance for Coventry City. He joined an exclusive group of 14 players to have exceeded three centuries of games for the club.

In a season when he was expected to take on a coaching role he found himself still called upon and made 36 appearances in 2004-05.

In his time with Coventry City Richard Shaw served under seven managers, not including caretaker-managers. He was also asked to play out of position at right back on many occasions and did so with gusto and professionalism, despite his dislike for the role.

Over some ten years of struggle, turmoil and dark times, Shaw has stuck with the Sky Blues and, in an era where loyalty is almost a forgotten virtue, has served with exceptional dedication. 1995-05. 335 apps. 1 goal.

SHEFFIELD WEDNESDAY CONNECTIONS
Continued from Sky Blue Heaven Vol I.
David Burrows (Coventry City March 1995-June 2000, 130 apps.) joined Wednesday via Birmingham City (free transfer) (Sheffield Wednesday March 2002-May 2003)
Terry Yorath (Coventry City player 1976-79, 107 apps.) was manager of Sheffield Wednesday from October 2001 until he resigned in October 2002.
Ex-Owls **Simon Donnelly** and **Phil O'Donnell** both appeared for Coventry during their pre-season tour of Germany in 2003. The trialists were not offered contracts.
Gavin Strachan had a trial at Sheffield Wednesday in March 2003. He left Coventry and after trials at Peterborough and Southend, joined Hartlepool United in August 2003. He later joined Halesowen Town.
Chris Marsden (on loan to Coventry 1993-94) played for Sheffield Wednesday in 2004-05.
Graham Barrett went on loan from Coventry City to Sheffield Wednesday in March 2005.
Veteran ex-Wednesday goalkeeper **Kevin Pressman** joined City as cover for Luke Steele in

March 2005, having been with Leicester City and Leeds United earlier in the season. He was released without having played a game.

Richie Partridge who was on loan at Coventry City 2002-03, joined Sheffield Wednesday at the start of 2005-06.

SHIRT SPONSORS

Shirt sponsorship was introduced in 1979.

1979-83	**TALBOT**
1983-84	No sponsor at start of season. **TALLON** from November.
1984-85	**GLAZEPTA**
1985-86	No sponsor at start of season. **ELLIOTS** from Spring
1986-88	**GRANADA SOCIAL CLUBS / GRANADA BINGO**
1988-89	None
1989-97	**PEUGEOT**
1997-05	**SUBARU** (home) / **ISUZU** (away)
2005-08	**CASSIDY GROUP**

SIMPSON, NOEL

Noel Simpson signed for City in August 1948 from Nottingham Forest for a £5,000 fee. He had spent five years at Forest and played for both Nottingham clubs during the war. He went on to captain the Coventry side for his last two seasons and was more or less an automatic choice in his eight and half years at Highfield Road.

Simpson was unfortunate to serve the club during a period when they were plummeting down the league and heading for Division Four. The "Boss" in Simpson's time at the club was any of the following managers: Billy Frith, Harry Storer, Jack Fairbrother, Charlie Elliott, Jesse Carver, George Raynor and Harry Warren. Despite that instability, he was a solid performer in a left wing half position.

In February 1957 at the age of 34, Noel was transferred to Exeter City. He ended his playing career there the following year. He returned to his native Nottinghamshire where he died from a heart attack whilst playing golf in 1987.
1948-57. 270 apps. 7 goals.

SOUTHERN LEAGUE

Coventry City played in the Southern League between 1908-1915. Their record is:

Southern League Division 1

	P	W	D	L	Pts	Final Pos
1908-09	40	15	4	21	34	20th
1909-10	42	19	8	15	46	8th
1910-11	38	16	6	16	38	10th
1911-12	38	17	8	13	42	6th
1912-13	38	13	8	17	34	13th
1913-14	38	6	14	18	26	20th*

Southern League Division 2.

	P	W	D	L	Pts	Final Pos
1914-15	24	13	2	9	28	5th

*Relegated.

Coventry City reserves played in the Southern League 1922-26.

ST. JOHN, IAN

Ian St. John is one of a small group of footballers, along with Bob Wilson and Gary Lineker, who have made the successful move to becoming a television sports presenter. "The Saint" (as he became known) has had a long career as a front-man on ITV Sport (as distinct from contributing as a pundit.)

Coventry City supporters might need reminding however, that Ian St. John was very briefly, a Sky Blue.

Scotsman St. John played for his home town club of Motherwell between 1958-61 before transferring to Liverpool. In the Shankly era, Ian was a key figure in the frontline. His 5'7" frame belied a terrific heading ability and goal poaching instinct.

Noel Cantwell (left) with Ian St John and his wife on the pitch at Highfield Road in 1971

He scored 118 goals in 426 matches during his ten years in a red shirt, winning the Championship twice and 21 Scotland caps. He scored the winning goal in the 1965 FA Cup Final, a header, as Liverpool beat Leeds United 2-1.

When Bill Shankly decided to release St. John in 1971, the player felt he still had something to offer at Liverpool, but he was 33-years-old by then. City

manager Noel Cantwell lured Ian to Highfield Road with a player/assistant-manager role. As well as adding experience to the Sky Blues young squad, St. John also got the opportunity to get on the property ladder.

The reality of football in the 1970s was that even a star name at a top club had been living in a club house in Merseyside. Liverpool wanted more money for the house than St. John could afford, so when he and his family moved to the midlands there were insufficient funds for their own home. The Coventry City director Phil Mead generously handed over a cheque for £3,000 to St. John, saying "pay me back when you can."

Ian St. John found himself at Highfield Road when the club were slipping down the table and memories of qualifying for Europe a long two years back. He made his City debut in a 1-0 win over Tottenham in September 1971 and then in his next game had a dream return to Merseyside scoring the winner in a 2-1 victory at Everton. In the next match at home to Leeds United, St. John inspired the Sky Blues to an impressive 3-1 victory with another goal.

City had won three in a row since St. John's arrival and his partnership with Willie Carr looked promising. It was a false dawn, however, and by February Coventry had won just twice in 17 games.

The Cantwell – St. John partnership came to an end abruptly in March 1972 when Cantwell was sacked. Ian St. John was offered the manager's role by the board, but he turned it down. His loyalty to Noel Cantwell made it impossible for him to accept the job. Ian played in just one game immediately after Cantwell's departure and left the club at the end of the season.

Ian St. John finished his playing career at Tranmere Rovers before moving into management. He was boss at Motherwell 1973-74, Portsmouth 1974-77 and was briefly assistant-manager at Sheffield Wednesday. The "Saint" joined Granada Television in 1978 and then presented "On the Ball" for LWT. In 1984 he teamed up with Jimmy Greaves for "Saint and Greavsie."

Nowadays Ian St. John does after-dinner speaking and in 2005, wrote his autobiography. He retains affection for the Sky Blues, but whether or not he'd have made a good manager of Coventry City, is something we'll never know.
20 Apps. 3 Goals. Player/Assistant-Manager 1971-72.

SUBSTITUTES
Coventry City's first substitute was Dietmar Bruck. The occasion was the home game at Highfield Road against Manchester City on September 4, 1965. Wearing shirt number 12, Bruck replaced Ron Farmer. The result was a 3-3 draw, with goals from Hudson, Clements and Farmer (pen.) Att. 29,403.

***

The first Coventry substitute to score was Bobby Gould, in City's second match in their inaugural Division One season, on August 22, 1967. The Coventry-born striker hit the net twice after he came on for George Curtis, who had been stretchered off with a broken leg. Curtis' injury had happened just four minutes into the game, and Gould's goals both came in the first half. The 3-3 draw was watched by a crowd of 44,950.

***

Coventry first brought on three substitutes in one game against Southampton at Highfield Road on October 10, 1996. Williams, Ndlovu and Dublin came on replacing Borrows, Burrows and Jess. Substitute Dublin grabbed a last minute goal to get the Sky Blues a 1-1 draw. The visitors made sure that the stadium announcer was kept busy, by also using all three of their substitutes. The ruling to allow three substitutes had been introduced in 1995-96, but City took their time to take full advantage.

Bobby Gould (left), City's first ever scoring substitute, enjoys breakfast with goalkeeper Bill Glazier (centre) and manager Jimmy Hill

***

The first City substitute to be sent off was Brian Borrows, against Newcastle United at St James Park on March 15, 1997. (Result L 0-4) Borrows came on at half-time and it was the only time that he was sent off in his career.

SUMMER TOURS

This is a list of City's out-of-season summer tours overseas. Note that Summer Tours up to the early 1990s were generally a reward at the end of a season. Since then they have become part of the pre-season build up.

1946   Denmark *four games*
1951   Netherlands *four games*
1962   West Germany *three games*
1963   West Germany *three games*
1965   Iceland *three games*
1966   Europe "Rover Car Tour" (West Germany, Austria, Switzerland & Belgium) *four games*
1967   West Indies *five games*
1968   Belgium *two games*
1969   West Indies (Barbados & Bermuda) *three games*

1970   USA *eight games*
1972   Far East (South Korea, Japan & Thailand) *six games*
1974   Malaysia & Singapore "Anchor Cup" v. Derby Co. (2x), v. Everton *three games. City won cup.*
1976   Sweden *two games*
1978   Japan "Japan Cup" v. Japan, v. Cologne, v. Palmeiras, v. Thailand *four games*
1981   South East Asia (Thailand, Malaysia, Hong Kong & Indonesia) *eight games*
1983   Zimbabwe *six games*
1984   Scandinavia (Sweden & Finland) *six games*
1990   Zimbabwe *three games*
1991   Spain *two games, end of season*
1992   Scotland *three games*
1993   Scotland *three games*
1994   Greece *two games, end of season* & West Country *three games pre-season*
1995   Portugal *two games*
1997   Scotland *three games*
1998   Scotland *two games*, Wales *two games*
1999   Germany *four games*
2000   Ireland *three games*
2001   Low Countries (Belgium & Netherlands) *three games*
2002   Germany (Nuremberg) *three games* & *three team mini tournament.*
2003   Germany *four games*
2004   Germany (Perl, Saarland) *three games* & *four team mini tournament.*
2005   Spain "Copa de Ibiza" v. Huddersfield T. v. QPR. & Ireland v. Athlone Town v. Galway Utd.
For one-off foreign matches see: Overseas Games.

TELFER, PAUL

Edinburgh-born Paul Telfer is the nephew of Falkirk boss Eamonn Bannon. He signed for Luton Town as a trainee in 1988 and was in the same team as former Sky Blue Trevor Peake and future City man John Hartson.

Paul Telfer

Telfer played a prominent role in David Pleat's side that reached the semi-finals of the FA Cup in 1994. In the season before he joined Coventry, midfielder Paul scored ten goals for the Hatters and had made more than 160 appearances for Luton when he left to join Coventry City.

Telfer was signed by Ron Atkinson in the summer of 1995 for a £1.15m. tribunal-set figure. Described by Trevor Peake as "a manager's dream" he was consistently praised by team-mates and managers alike as a model professional. With a terrific engine, he was strong in the air and provided good delivery with his passing game and from dead ball kicks.

In only his second match for the club, Telfer scored in a 2-1 win over Manchester City. A month or so later, in September 1995, Coventry turned down the chance to double their money, rejecting an offer of £3m. from Blackburn Rovers.

During the 1997-98 season, Telfer scored two important goals in the FA Cup run, the second at Sheffield United in the sixth round replay, a long range drive following a free kick. He also scored a goal at Crystal Palace in the league, less than a minute into the match, enjoying an advanced midfield role in Gary McAllister's absence through injury.

It was a long time coming but Paul finally won a full Scotland cap against World Champions France on March 29, 2000 at Hampden Park at the age of 28. Playing at right back, he was in the starting line-up, although the Scots lost 0-2.

The move to right back during 1999-00 showed his versatility and, while he may have been unspectacular Telfer rarely let the side down in his six seasons at the club. Indeed, he sometimes went beyond the call of duty and played while injured. In the last few games of the 2000-01 season, Paul played with a fractured cheekbone, then broke his leg in the match at Aston Villa in April 2001 which sealed Coventry's relegation. He would not play for the Sky Blues again.

Once recovered he re-joined Gordon Strachan at Southampton on October 31, 2001 on a free transfer and then reunited with Strachan again in the summer of 2005 when his former boss took over at Celtic.
1995-01. 226 Apps. 12 Goals.

TESTIMONIALS, AWAY

Coventry City were the guest team or star attraction at the following testimonials:

v Southport – *Ray Minshull, Al Barratt and Wally Taylor.* May 2, 1956. Att. 3,202. Result W 4-2. Scorers: Uphill, Hill P., Sambrook (2). *A "Benefit Match" for three players in one go.*

v Ilkeston – *Terry Swinscoe.* May 11, 1966. Att. 600. Result D 4-4. Scorers: Farmer, Roberts, Pointer, Clements.

v Nuneaton Borough – *Malcolm Allen and Roger Thompson.* May 15, 1967. Att. 7,250. Result W 7-3.

Scorers: Tudor (4), Machin, Farmer, Gibson. *"Grand Challenge Match" for two long-serving Boro players. John Tudor hit a hat-trick in four minutes and three minutes later scored his fourth.*

v Aston Villa – *Charlie Aitken.* April 20, 1970. Att. 9,512. Result 3-3. Scorers: Rafferty, O'Rourke, Machin. *George Curtis was a Villa player at the time and played against Coventry.*

v Derby County – *Ron Webster.* March 24, 1971. Att. 9,318. Result L.1-2. Scorer: Rafferty. *Ron Webster is nowadays a cattle farmer in Derbyshire.*

v Oxford United – *Graham Atkinson.* May 7, 1973. Att. 4,000. Result W 2-1. Scorers: Cartwright, Ferguson. *Chelsea stars Peter Osgood and Alan Hudson played for Oxford in a game for "Big Ron's" brother.*

v Nottingham Forest – *Peter Hindley.* October 29, 1974. Result 1-1. Scorer: Cross. *Hindley played for both sides during his career. He is nowadays a painter and decorator in Peterborough.*

v Nantes (France) – *Bernard Blanchet.* May 20, 1975. Att. 5,000. Result L 0-2. *Blanchet was a one club man and played 17 times for France, scoring 5 goals, between 1966-72.*

v Exeter City – *Keith Harvey.* September 2, 1975. Result D 2-2. Scorers: Cross, Ferguson. *New signing Barry Powell made his first appearance in Sky Blue.*

v. Grimsby Town – *Dave Boylen.* November 17, 1975. Att. 3,655. Result 3-3. Scorers: Coop, Murphy (2).

v Millwall – *Bryan King.* April 30, 1976. Result L 1-2. Scorer: Cross. *Match abandoned 12 minutes before the end - fans on pitch.*

v Nuneaton Borough – *David Lewis.* May 23, 1977. Att. 1,466. Result L 0-1. *City's team included a number of first team regulars including Jim Holton, Ian Wallace and Tommy Hutchison.*

v Brighton & Hove Albion – *Chris Cattlin.* August 9, 1977. Att. 8,918. Result L 1-3. Scorer: Coop (pen.) *A number of Sky Blues fans made the trip to the Goldstone Ground for this benefit match. Prior to the game, Cattlin expressed his dislike for games not taken seriously. Brighton manager Alan Mullery declared, "We don't play friendlies." Coventry took them at their word and in a bruising encounter Brighton had three players* carried off. Mark Lawrenson scored one of the Brighton goals. Cattlin went on to manage the Sussex side between 1983-86.

v Leicester City – *Steve Whitworth.* November 6, 1979. Att. 3,402. Result L 1-3. Scorer: Hateley. *The away dressing room was more crowded than the stadium, as Coventry made eight substitutions at half time and one more later. A total of 20 Coventry players got a game.*

v Wimbledon – *David Clement.* March 26, 1983. Att. 895. Result 1-1. Scorer: Hendrie. *Memorial game for the former England and QPR player who had died shortly before he was due to take a coaching job at Wimbledon.*

v Bristol Rovers – *Steve Bailey.* November 15, 1983. Att. 1,859. Result W 2-1. Scorers: Hunt, Withey.

v. Hereford United – *Steve Emery.* July 25, 1987. Att. 4,000. Result L 1-2. Scorer: Sedgley. *The Sky Blues pay a visit to manager John Sillett's former club as FA Cup holders.*

v Walsall – *Kenny Mower.* July 28, 1987. Att. 4,450. Result 0-0. *Mower made almost 500 apps. for the Saddlers. City paraded the FA Cup before the game - a preparation for the Charity Shield match v. Everton at Wembley. A very rare, scoreless testimonial.*

v. Plymouth Argyle – *Leigh Cooper.* August 19, 1988. Att. 5,037. Result W 2-1. Scorers: Speedie, Bannister. *Leigh Cooper played almost 400 games for Plymouth. He has since managed Truro, Holsworthy and Saltash United in Cornwall. John Uzzell (see below) came on as a substitute for Plymouth.*

v Bristol Rovers – *Ray Kendall.* May 9, 1994. Result 2-2. Scorers: Atherton, Darby. *Kendall was Rovers' long-serving kit man. City left afterwards for a ten day tour to Greece.*

v Heart of Midlothian – *Craig Levein.* October 8, 1995. Att. 3,500. Result W 5-1. Scorers: Ndlovu (2),

Chris Cattlin

Salako (2), Lamptey. *Levein, a long-serving player at Tynecastle, went on to manage Hearts for four years before becoming manager of Leicester City in October 2004.*

v West Bromwich Albion – *Stuart Naylor.* May 6, 1996. Result L 2-3. Scorers: Salako, o.g.

v Hibernian – *Gordon Hunter.* September 9, 1996. Att. 5,353. Result L 2-3. Scorers: Richardson, Telfer. *The Edinburgh Evening News stated that City manager Gordon Strachan promised to parade a "galaxy of stars" from the "Premiership big spenders." He also fulfilled a boyhood dream by playing for Hibernian and scored a penalty for Hibs to win. Ray Wilkins played for Coventry City adding to the stellar line-up.*

v Torquay United – *John Uzzell.* August 1, 1997. Att. 1,268. Result W 4-1. Scorers: Dublin (2), McAllister, Salako. *Uzzell was forced to retire from football when he suffered an horrendous facial injury after a clash with Gary Blissett in a game against Brentford. Uzzell had to have a metal plate and a plastic eye socket fitted but was unsuccessful in a court case claim for assault*

v St. Johnstone – *Roddy Grant.* November 12, 1999. Att. 2,638. Result L 2-3. Scorers: McAllister, Eustace. *City sent a full squad, other than players on international duty, to McDiarmid Park, Perth.*

v Worcester City – *Carl Heeley.* March 25, 2005. Att. 624. Result W 5-1. Scorers: Johnson (2), Morrell, Wood, O'Toole. *Heeley had made 513 appearances for the Conference North league side. A few weeks later, having failed to agree terms, Heeley left to join Hinckley United.*

TESTIMONIALS HOME
(Continued from Sky Blue Heaven Vol I)
Michael Gynn.
CITY 1987 XI v ALL STARS XI.
April 19, 2005. Att. 9,435. Result 7-7. Scorers: (City 87)

Gynn (19 pen & 52), Regis (31), Busst o.g. (61), Keys (69), Culpin (72), Borrows (89); (All Stars) Rush (17), Bull (21,57,71,75), Walters (35 & 78).

City 87 XI:
Steve Ogrizovic, Brian Borrows, Lloyd McGrath, Trevor Peake, Greg Downs, Micky Gynn, Dave Phillips, Dave Bennett, Cyrille Regis, David Speedie, Tommy Hutchison. Subs Used: Steve Sedgley, Graham Rodger, Tim Flowers, Kevan Smith, Dean Emerson, Steve Collins, Paul Culpin, Richard Keys.

All Stars XI:
Dale Belford, Neil Pointon, Dave Busst, Micky Thomas, Mark Walters, Steve Hodge, Gordon Cowans, Liam Brady, Steve Bull, Ian Rush, Chris Waddle. Subs Used: Mick Quinn, Clive Allen, Tony Morley.

UNSUNG HEROES

Bert Edwards was one of the longest serving people in the club's history. A former player with Torquay United, he was an FA qualified coach with a speciality in body development.

Bert was with Exeter City from 1962 to 1967, when he joined Barnsley. He came to Coventry City in 1970 as the club's physical trainer. In 1972 he was appointed as reserve team coach with responsibilities for the youth side

Following the retirement of Bob Dennison in the summer of 1978, Edwards moved from youth coach to become controller of scouting and youth recruitment. Among the players he helped through to the first team were Garry Thompson, Andy Blair, Mark Hateley, Gary Bannister, Danny Thomas and Steve Sedgely.

In 1981 John Sillett joined his team of coaches alongside Colin Dobson. In the mid-1980s, Bert left the club for a period of 14 months, but when Sillett became manager, he brought Edwards back into the fold. Bert's job title changed over the years, although his main focus remained with the youth set-up at the Ryton training camp into the 1990s. Bert was a father figure to many of the young lads at Ryton.

He said of his role, "I've had a job in a million – the sort of job anyone interested in football would want. To recruit kids at 13 or 14 and then watch them come through to make the grade gives you a hell of a lot of satisfaction."

In the summer of 1995 Bert's role was re-defined as recruitment officer. Tragically, Bert Edwards died while still working at the club on December 3, 1995, at age of 67.

John Sillett's tribute to him at the time was, "Bert's death is a real tragedy. He gave his heart and soul to Coventry City for many years. He could judge a player very well and not many people have the ability to do that." Bert Edwards had served the club for more than 22 years.

***

Dick Hill was trainer at Coventry City from 1935 to 1949. In a 14 year period spanning either side of World War Two, he worked at the club during both Harry Storer's and Billy Frith's first periods as managers and was always to be seen in team photographs.

Hill had a long career in football. As a player, he won a cap for England against Belgium in May 1926. He played for Millwall and Torquay United, ending his career at Newark Town. He also played for the Army while serving with the Grenadier Guards.

He was trainer at Mansfield Town before joining Coventry City. He returned to Torquay United to work as trainer before retiring. He died in 1971.

***

As a college lecturer and educationalist, **Jack Leavers** would seem to be an unlikely candidate for a Sky Blues hero. However, Jack was involved with Coventry City for a great many years in a number of roles.

Jack's connection to the club began in 1954 when he invited City players to do some football coaching at Woodlands Comprehensive school, where he was head of engineering and science. In 1962 the link to the club became stronger. Manager Jimmy Hill invited Jack to coach the Coventry "C" teams, the three youth sides.

Jack Leavers

While young players came through the ranks, Leavers insisted on their pursuing qualifications along the way. Among those who were later grateful for Jack's input, were Willie Carr, Dennis Mortimer and Mick McGuire. They all took extra exams and in McGuire's case, he went on to take a degree. He is now an executive with the Professional Footballers Association.

Jack Leavers was never full-time with Coventry City yet he worked as education officer, youth coach, gateman, barman, crowd packer, and general factotum. Jack also did some scouting for the club and would often be seen at the Ryton Training ground in his spare time encouraging the youngsters.

He moved into further education at Coventry Technical College and ultimately became principal lecturer at Brooklands Annexe, and when he retired in April 1997 at the age of 77 a surprise party was thrown for him. Those who came along to pay tribute included Peter Hill, Dietmar Bruck, Bobby Gould, Brian Roberts, Trevor Gould, George Curtis and Gerry Baker, in addition to the three players mentioned earlier.

***

Bill Trew was boot man at Ryton for more than 11 years. Bill celebrated his 79th birthday on New Years Day 1978 and was still working on keeping the boots clean. "I must have cleaned thousands of boots since I arrived here." An essential "backroom boy" at the club, Bill said wet weather posed his biggest problem, when he had to dry the boots in the boiler house.

***

Pat Saward was with City for seven years and was enormously influential in the Sky Blue era. Although born in Cobh, Ireland, Saward's father travelled with his job, so Pat had lived in Singapore and Malta before the family settled in south London.

Saward began his playing career at Millwall, but had his greatest success at Aston Villa, winning the FA Cup in 1957.

Pat Seward

He was an Eire international and was often a team mate of his future boss, Noel Cantwell. Following a time at Huddersfield Town, he was offered player-manager jobs at Exeter and Chester but he chose to return to the Midlands and joined Third Division Coventry as player-coach in 1963.

Known as "The Duke" by colleagues for his immaculate dress, Saward earned a terrific reputation for his work with young players. When

Noel Cantwell was appointed manager in 1967, one of his first acts was to make Pat Saward his assistant manager. Saward continued with the youth players and in 1968 City reached the final of the Youth Cup.

Among the players who he brought forward were Willie Carr, Mick Coop, Jimmy Holmes, Jeff Blockley and Dennis Mortimer.
Saward was on Coventry's books as a player and made appearances for the reserves, but he was never called upon to play for the first team.

With a growing reputation as a coach, Pat Saward was lured away to manage a club for himself. In June 1970 he joined Brighton and Hove Albion. Two years later they were promoted to the Second Division, but he was sacked in October 1973.

Saward coached in Saudi Arabia during the late 1970s. He ran a business in Minorca before returning to England and spent his final years living in Newmarket, where he passed away in 2002, aged 74.

***

Colin Dobson had three spells with Coventry City on the coaching side and is highly regarded as one of the best youth coaches in football. Dobson had a distinguished playing career.

He made 200 appearances for Sheffield Wednesday and played for England under-23s in 1963, making his debut alongside another debutant, Ernie Hunt, later to become a Sky Blues favourite.

After nine years at Hillsborough, Dobson joined Huddersfield Town in 1966. He was Town's top scorer in the 1966-67 season and a member of the Division Two promotion side of 1970.

Following a time on the coaching staff at Bristol Rovers, Dobson first joined the Sky Blues in September 1977 as Youth Coach under Gordon Milne. The responsibility for the reserves was also part of his remit.

In 1981, the Youth coaching came under John Sillett's wing and Dobson concentrated on the reserves. Dobson left in 1983 and coached a club side in Bahrain. He moved on two years later to Qatar to work under the managership of former City assistant manager Alan Dicks.

Having finished his spell in the Persian Gulf, Colin returned to England in 1986. After two years coaching at Aston Villa, Dobson was on his travels again to work under Keith Burkinshaw at Sporting Lisbon. He returned with Burkinshaw in 1989 to work at Gillingham for a year. Still based in Coventry despite his travels, his next job came by accident.

While Dobson was out running one day in 1990, City manager John Sillett drove past him on a country lane and stopped his car. He offered him a return to the Sky Blues as youth coach.

Colin's second stay lasted two years until he was invited back to the Gulf. This time it was to Kuwait and then Oman.

Colin Dobson returned to Ryton for his third term with Coventry City in 1999. He joined the academy team of coaches, teaching the under-11s during the day and the academy youngsters in the evenings. He has now left the club and is currently chief scout at Stoke City.

***

By the time **Bob Dennison** joined Coventry City he had accumulated a wealth of football experience. He had become known as football's

"Mr. Discovery" for his talent at finding good young players.

Bob managed Northampton Town from 1948 until he became manager of Middlesbrough in July 1954. Bob discovered Brian Clough in his time with Boro and he also signed an 18-year-old Ian Gibson from Bradford Park Avenue, later to star at Coventry.

Alf Walton

After eight years at Ayresome Park, Bob was sacked and spent nearly a year out of football before he joined Southern League Hereford. He moved from Hereford in December 1967 when manager Noel Cantwell asked him to join Coventry City as Chief Scout.

Bob Dennison

Among the players he brought to the club were Jimmy Holmes, Danny Thomas, Mark Hateley, Andy Blair and Garry Thompson.

When Cantwell was sacked in March 1972, Dennison took over as caretaker-manager. He was in charge to the end of the season and City achieved safety from relegation.

After the appointment of the new management team Joe Mercer and Gordon Milne in June 1972, Bob continued at the club as assistant manager. Despite the job title, Dennison reverted to his role as the club's Chief Scout. Having not been in the best of health for some months, Bob retired from Coventry City in the summer of 1978 after almost 11 years full-time service at the club. However, he continued scouting for the club for many years from his Kent home. Bob Dennison died in 1996.

***

Lancashire scout **Alf Walton** trawled the schools pitches of the North West from his home in Bury. He was not able to watch any games anonymously as his six feet-plus stature stood out somewhat.

His task was not made any easier as he didn't drive a car and travelled everywhere by bus and train to seek out the talent. A final hurdle was that whenever Alf saw a useful youngster, he faced enormous competition from the big clubs in his area – the Liverpool and Manchester teams for example.

It is to his credit, therefore, that Alf discovered and persuaded some notable youngsters to join the club. Ernie Machin, Graham Paddon, Dennis Mortimer, Alan Dugdale and Mick Maguire were amongst those Alf Walton discovered.

***

A groundsman at Highfield Road, **Ellick Smith** was a servant to the club for a long time. He broke his leg in two places on February 18, 1963 slipping on ice, in the big freeze. Having recovered from that he was given some help in his task when pitch slope was levelled in summer of 1963.

In March 1969, Smith was, as the club put it, "having to take a back seat." Perhaps not the luckiest of people, he'd fallen off some scaffolding just before the Sheffield Wednesday match and suffered three cracked ribs. Smith was still ill in hospital in April 1971.

***

Gordon Pettifer, the groundsman at Ryton

training ground, first joined Coventry City in 1968 when Noel Cantwell was manager. After 3½ years he left and worked at other sports grounds in Coventry over the next nine years.

In 1980 he returned to the club with responsibility for four full-sized pitches and two smaller pitches at the training camp. He was at the club in all weathers until his retirement in the summer of 2002 at the age of 64. In his two spells at Coventry City he had worked for some 25 and a half years.

***

The longest serving employee at Coventry City is manager's secretary **Jenny Poole**, who began her 37th. year with the club in May 2005. Jenny first arrived at the club as a temp, filling in for Rose McNulty (Sky Blue Rose) for two weeks in 1968. When a full-time vacancy arose Jenny jumped at the chance to stay on. Initially she worked as secretary to the stadium manager Neil Solman doubling up as a receptionist at Highfield Road.

Jenny Poole

Before long she was asked to become manager Noel Cantwell's secretary and stayed in that role through the many managerial changes ever since. The manager's office was located at Highfield Road up to 1980, but when the new facilities were built at Ryton, the offices of manager and secretary moved to the Sky Blue Lodge.

Jenny has been secretary to every manager from Cantwell to Micky Adams. When asked who was her favourite ever Coventry manager, Jenny, the very epitome of discretion, named each one of the managers she has worked with. They number 19.

***

Trevor Gould was a player and youth team coach at the club for a total of some 18 years. The younger brother of Bobby, Coventry-born Trevor was an England Schoolboy international. He joined the City youth team and made nine league appearances in the 1969-70 season.

Trevor Gould

Trevor didn't get any more chances at Highfield Road and was released in October 1970, joining Northampton Town.

He made more than 100 appearances for the Cobblers before moving to Bedford Town in 1973. Gould was voted Player of the Year three times before becoming player-manager in August 1978.

When the Bedford club folded in 1982, he joined Rushden and after a year moved on to manage Aylesbury Town in July 1983. Gould enjoyed tremendous success with the Southern League side, winning the Championship in 1987-88. The reward for the club was a rare friendly game when Aylesbury faced the full England team managed by Bobby Robson.

In 1992 Trevor re-joined Coventry City as youth team coach. He helped unearth players including Willie Boland, Barry Quinn, Marcus Hall, Chris Kirkland, John Eustace and Gary McSheffrey. Gould worked closely at Ryton with Brian Roberts and, more recently, academy manager Steve Ogrizovic and his assistant Brian Borrows.

After 13 years as a coach, youth development officer and director of youth, Gould left the club in June 2005.

Despite being made redundant due to cutbacks, Gould held no hard feelings on leaving the club. "I had five years as a player and 13 happy years as a coach. I have seen a lot of lads progress up through the ranks and it is always a great pleasure to see them reach the first team.

"I am proud to have set up the business plan for the academy and help get the club to two FA Youth Cup finals and this year's play-off finals where we unfortunately lost out to Blackburn Rovers. I just hope the club retain their academy status now."

Regarded as one of the nicest men in football, the 55-year-old planned to take a break with his family before hoping to get another job in the game.

VARIOUS ODDS AND ENDS

Coventry hold the record for the biggest win with a depleted side, that is, with ten men, before the advent of substitutes. They won 7-1 against Aldershot on Sep. 22, 1958 even though goalkeeper Jim Sanders went off with a broken leg with 20 minutes to play. Roy Kirk pulled on the keeper's jersey.

***

In 1959 George Curtis combined playing for Coventry City with doing his national service. Curtis was stationed with an RAF unit at Bridgnorth. In September he was given late permission to play at Halifax and joined his team-mates with three hours notice.

He returned to his unit after the 2-2 draw, but the following Friday manager Billy Frith drove to Bridgnorth to ask for Curtis' release. George still

had a month to go to complete his basic training, but he managed to change his cookhouse duty to be able to play, and City beat Swindon 3-1.

***

The club's first ever game in Sky Blue colours was against Birmingham City on August 10, 1962. The kit was an instant hit as Hugh Barr scored 30 seconds after kick-off. The "Public Charity Match" at St Andrew's was attended by 9,229 and City won 2-1 with a winner by Terry Bly.

***

By the time Coventry City had secured the Division Two Championship in April 1967, George Curtis had become a legend at the club. He was awarded a testimonial game which jointly honoured Mick Kearns. The opponents were a full strength Liverpool side.

"Iron Man" George obviously had no intention that the game would be treated as a friendly. Within minutes of the kick-off, Curtis performed a crunching tackle on Ian St.John. The Liverpool man recalled, "I woke up being carried off on a stretcher. When I challenged him (Curtis) later about the tackle, he said: 'It's a man's game, Saint,' and that from a man we were down trying to make a few bob for!"

***

Neil Martin, Coventry City centre forward between 1968 and 1971, had been about to quit football in his early days in Scotland. A former coal miner, he planned to become a long distance lorry driver when he was persuaded to stay in the game by George Farm, his manager at Queen of the South. He later moved to Hibernian, where his career took off.

***

In January 1970 goalkeeper Bill Glazier enquired into the possibility of representing Eire as an International player. Both of Bill's parents were born in Dublin so he qualified on that basis. However, the application was rejected by FIFA as

"Iron Man" George Curtis (right) relaxing with Ron Farmer (centre) and Alan Dicks

Glazier had already played for the England U-23 side.

***

City failed to win against a team without a recognised goalkeeper in December 1971. Chelsea held out for a 1-1 draw at Stamford Bridge for a whole hour after Peter Bonetti was carried off. Defender David Webb put on the gloves and a goal from Willie Carr was the only effort that passed the stand-in keeper.

***

Larry Lloyd is one of just 12 men to have won the League Championship (now the Premiership) with two clubs. Unfortunately for Coventry City fans, the clubs were Liverpool in 1973 and Nottingham Forest in 1978 and not the Sky Blues. His Championships sandwiched his time at Highfield Road (City player 1974-76).

One of the other players to have won the Championship at two clubs is Kevin Richardson (City player 1995-97). His title winning clubs were Everton (1985) and Arsenal (1989).

***

Bill Glazier could have played for the Republic of Ireland, but was prevented by FIFA

The Sky Blues have won a cup-tie by the "away goals ruling" just once. In the 1982-83 League Cup match against Fulham, the aggregate score was 2-2 after a 0-0 draw at home. City went through to the third round on the basis of scoring twice in the away leg, the away goals counting double in the event of an aggregate draw. It has never happened since.

**

Former Coventry City player Nii Lamptey may hold the record for playing club football in more countries than anyone else. The Ghana international first played for Anderlecht in Belgium, having joined them as a 15-year-old, then had a season on loan to PSV Eindhoven in the Netherlands before arriving in Britain at Aston Villa. He made his only move between clubs of one country when Ron Atkinson signed the 20-year-old for the Sky Blues in 1995.

After leaving City (1995-96 11 apps. 2 goals) he really became a nomad and played in Italy for Venezia, Union de Santa Fe in Argentina, Ankaragucu in Turkey (1992-98), Uniao Leiria in Portugal, Greuther Fürth in Germany (1999-01) and lastly Shandong Lunang in China (2001-02). At the latest count, that brings the total to nine countries.

Television stardom and Coventry City do not normally get mentioned in the same sentence. Jimmy Hill of course, is a veteran of "Match of the Day" and other programmes. Several City managers and players have appeared on "A Question of Sport."

Dion Dublin and Gary McAllister, for example, have been both guests and "mystery personalities." McAllister also made a brief showing on "This is Your Life" honouring Eddie Jordan, a fan of the Sky Blues. Both Gordon Strachan and Peter Reid have appeared as "experts" or "pundits" on the BBC at live games.

The closest to achieve "fame" on the box may be Cobi Jones. The USA International, who played briefly for the Sky Blues, hosted his own show "MTV Mega-Dose" a special on health and fitness. More theatrically, he made a guest appearance on the teen soap Beverley Hills 90210 in 1994. (see also: Arm Wrestling, Monty Python)

***

Arsenal manager Arsene Wenger is reported to have lost his temper only twice – at Old Trafford when Man United beat them 5-2 and when the Gunners were beaten by Coventry City 3-2 on Boxing Day in 1999.

Some of the Arsenal squad are reported to have accused team-mate Marc Overmars of not trying, in what is known at Highbury as "The Coventry Row."

***

A double connection between Coventry City and the England national team occurred when Noel Cantwell was employed in a scouting capacity in 1999. The former City manager had been out of the game for several years when another ex-Coventry boss, Dave Sexton, brought him into the FA set-up.

WALES INTERNATIONALS

The following Coventry City players represented Wales. (First figure: caps while playing with Coventry. Total apps. in brackets. + indicates still playing.)

R.O. Bob Evans	5 (9)	1911-12
Leslie Jones	5 (11)	1935-37
George Lowrie	3 (4)	1947-48
Bryn Allen	2 (2)	1950
Ronnie Rees	21 (39)	1964-68
Les Cartwright	5 (7)	1974-76
Terry Yorath	20 (59)	1976-79
Donato Nardiello	2 (2)	1977
David Phillips	9 (62)	1987-89
Simon Haworth	4 (5)	1997-98
John Hartson	4 (37+)	2001
Craig Bellamy	3 (21+)	2000-01
David Pipe	1 (1)	2003
Robert Page	4 (40+)	2005-

Paul Trollope 1 cap (9) - *Fulham (on loan to City) 2002.* **Richard Duffy** 2 caps (2) – *Portsmouth (on loan to City) 2004-06.* International debut v. Slovenia August 17, 2005.

● Bobby Gould, the former Sky Blues player and twice manager, was manager of Wales from August 1995-June 1999.

● Terry Yorath was manager of Wales from April 1988-November 1993.

WAR

"There is only time for one thing now and that is war. If the cricketer has a straight eye let him look along the barrel of a rifle. If a footballer has strength of limb let him serve and march in the field of battle." Sir Arthur Conan Doyle. Recruiting speech, September 6, 1914.

***

"No British troops ever travel without footballs or the energy to kick them." General Jack, 1917.

Coventry City players have fought in both World Wars.

FIRST WORLD WAR 1914-18

Initially following the outbreak of the Great War in 1914, competitive football continued. Coventry City played games in the Southern League Division Two, until the end of the 1914-15 season. The hostilities prevented any further organised sport. Many Coventry City players joined the Army and were involved in the fighting.

The following players lost their lives in the First World War:

John Harkins: As a soldier with the Royal Highlanders "Black Watch" Regiment, Scotsman Harkins was bought out of the Army by Middlesbrough in 1906.

He played for several clubs before signing for Coventry in May 1914. After one season in the Southern League, he re-joined the Army in 1915. He subsequently lost his life and is buried at the Amara War Cemetery in Iraq. (1914-15. 18 apps. 1 goal)

Steve Jackson: He joined the Army early in the War becoming a Sergeant Major in the South Staffs Regiment. He received the M.M. and D.C.M. (for distinguished conduct in the field). He was killed in action on October 26, 1917. (1911-14. 13 apps.)

F. Walter Kimberley: He enlisted early in the conflict in August 1914, joining the 1st. Battalion Coldstream Guards. He was originally reported as killed in action but was captured and held as a prisoner of war. He died on return to England on April 22, 1917. (1912-14. 23 apps. 1 goal)

Tom Morris: He played for City for less than one season, joining the Army in March 1915. he was later killed in action. (1914-15. 19 apps. 2 goals)

Jack Tosswill: He joined the Royal Engineers as a Corporal in the summer of 1914, but was killed in action on September 28, 1915. (1913-14. 17 apps. 1 goal)

George "Tubby" Warren: He had four seasons at Coventry City but by the time war broke out he was playing for Nuneaton. He enlisted in February 1917 and served with the 2nd Battalion York and Lancaster Regiment. He was killed in France on May 17, 1917. George Warren is buried in Philosophe British Cemetery, Mazingarbe. (1907-11. 109 apps. 56 goals).

The following players were wounded during the First World War:

Jerry Best *236 apps. See Best, Jerry.*

Stanley Day *On club books but never played.*

R.O. Bob Evans *139 apps.*

Eli Juggins *Moved to Southampton FC shortly before the outbreak of hostilities, then served with the Cheshire Regiment. Injured, he was in the military hospital at Audregnies before returning to Coventry as ground superintendent in April 1919. (111 apps. 7 goals).*

Walter Wilson: *Enlisted in March 1914 and served*

with the King's Own Scottish Borderers in France. He was badly injured and awarded the M.M. (4 app.).

Billy Yates: *111 apps. 1 goal.*

Also Served:

Bob Alderson: *Served with the Tyne Electrical Engineers as a Sergeant. (15 apps. 3 goals).*

John Doran: *Played just once for City before enlisting. Serving with the R.A.O.C. Doran was awarded both the D.C.M. and M.M. After the war he played for several clubs, including Norwich City and Manchester City. (1 app. 2 goals).*

Joe Enright: *Served with the R.A.O.C. until 1919, when he returned to his home country of Ireland. (22 apps. 9 goals).*

Patsy Hendren: *Joined the 1st Sportsman's Battalion (23rd. Royal Fusiliers) which had been formed on September 25, 1914. (33 apps. 14 goals). See Cricketers.*

Tom Shields: *4 apps.*

Charlie Tickle: *125 apps. 21 goals.*

Robert Turner: *14 apps. 1 goal*

SECOND WORLD WAR 1939-45.

No Coventry City players were killed during the Second World War. Sadly, one former player was to lose his life, **Arthur Bacon.** A Coventry City player between 1934-37 (16 apps. 17 goals), Bacon had a stunning but short-lived Coventry career scoring more than a goal a game. He was forced to leave City after suffering an eye injury and signed for Burton Town. Bacon was killed in an air raid in Hawthorn Street, Derby on July 27, 1942, after he fell off his bicycle while serving as a special constable.

Also Served:

Jack Astley: *Retired from playing during the war, and joined the Army as an officer. (1936-44. 140 apps. 5 goals). He remained with the services after hostilities ended.*

Ken Chisholm: *(1950-52. 71 apps. 35 goals) was an RAF fighter pilot.*

Lol Coen: *Played for City either side of the war 1938-48 (22 apps. 3 goals). During the war he made guest appearances for several clubs and was awarded the D.F.C.*

Ernie Curtis: *Played for Coventry at the end of a career that had included an FA Cup winners medal with Cardiff City. An ex-Wales international, Curtis was with Coventry between 1935-37 (21 apps. 2 goals). He served in the Far East in the war and was taken prisoner by the Japanese 1941-45. He returned to his home town Cardiff, where he died in 1992 at the age of 85.*

Don Dorman: *A City player from 1951-54 (94 apps. 32 goals) he had served in the war before becoming a professional footballer. He was twice wounded and was captured in the battle of Arnhem.*

Charlie Elliott: *Joined the Navy towards the end of the war (101 apps. 2 goals). See cricketers.*

Jim Harrison: *Served in India and Burma with the Army (23 apps. 3 goals).*

Martin McDonnell: *Served in Normandy at the end of the war (245 apps.).*

Ted Roberts: *Played for Coventry City either side of the war, 1936-39 & 1946-52 (223 apps. 87 goals). Roberts fought at Arnhem in 1944.*

Key: D.C.M. *Distinguished Conduct Medal* M.M. *Military Medal* D.F.C. *Distinguished Flying Cross* R.A.O.C. *Royal Army Ordnance Corps*

***

Mo Konjic was one Coventry City player with experience of a modern war. He spent over eight months as a soldier with the Bosnian Army. During the conflict his eponymous home village south west of Sarajevo was flattened.

He finally secured a transfer from FC Sarajevo to Croatian club NK Zagreb while the war continued. Conditions were so bad that the fee was paid in food and his wages were food parcels. He nearly didn't make it to his new club.

With the war still raging in the Balkans, Konjic and a friend as driver, set off north through the mountains. Because of the road-blocks they chose a route that used forest tracks and mountain roads. It was a two day drive and at some point the driver fell asleep at the wheel. The car hit a bus and plunged down a ravine.
Mo broke both arms in the crash. Two weeks later he played in a match in extreme pain.

"I had to play because my family needed food. I was

Mo Konjic

crying every time I made a tackle or jumped for a header. The other players didn't know why I was crying because they didn't know about my broken arms."
Following Zagreb, Konjic played in Switzerland for FC Zurich before making a £2.2million. transfer to Monaco in 1996. While in the French league side he played in the Champions league and was in the Monaco side that beat Manchester United at the quarter-final stage.

Mo joined Coventry from Monaco in 1999 and England became the fifth country he had played football in. The 6'4" (1.93m.) Bosnian was very popular with the City faithful between January 1999 and May 2004 (155 apps. 4 goals), when he was transferred to Derby County.

He played for Derby against City in the very last match at Highfield Road, April 30, 2005.

WHAT IF?

1 The Second World War had not started just as City were looking favourites for promotion to Division One?
2 Brian Clough had succeeded Jimmy Hill in October 1967, instead of turning down the job?
3 Malcolm Allison had joined on either of the occasions he was alleged to have been offered a job as Coventry coach, October 1967 and February 1969?
4 Kevin Keegan had been taken on

as a Coventry player instead of being rejected for a lack of height?

5 Dennis Mortimer had not been sold in 1975?

6 Arsenal had beaten Ipswich Town in the 1978 FACup Final and the Sky Blues had qualified for the UEFA Cup?

7 Coventry had been allowed to play in the European Cup Winners Cup in 1987-88?

8 Robbie Keane had not been sold?

9 Craig Bellamy had not missed so many goalscoring opportunities in the season City were relegated?

10 Eric Black had been kept on as manager?

WINS

BIGGEST LEAGUE WINS HOME (1919 onwards):

9-0 v Bristol C Division 3(S) Apr 28 1934 Bourton (4), Jones (2), White (2), Lauderdale.

8-0 v Crystal Palace Division 3(S) Feb 6 1932 Bourton (3), Lauderdale (2), Lake, White, Holmes.

8-1 v Crystal Palace Division 3(S) Nov 9 1935 Bourton (3), Jones (2), McNestry (2), Lauderdale.

8-1 v Shrewsbury Town Division 3 Oct 22 1963 Rees (3), Hudson (2), Barr (2) og.

7-0 v QPR Division 3(S) Mar 4 1933 Lake (3), Bourton (2), Lauderdale, Richards.

7-1 v Wolves Division 2 Dec 25 1922 Toms (3) Richmond (2), Jones, Wood.

7-1 v Rotherham U Division 3(N) Nov 7 1925 Herbert (3), Paterson (2), Dougall, Poole.

7-1 v Thames Division 3(S) Sep 23 1930 Richards (2), Lake, Phillips, Ball og (2).

7-1 v Gillingham Division 3(S) Aug 26 1933 Bourton (2), Lauderdale (2), Lake (2), Richards.

7-1 v Newport C Division 3(S) Sep 7 1935 Bourton (3) Jones (2) Lauderdale (2)

7-1 v Aldershot Division 4 Sep 22 1958 Rogers (4), Shaw (3).

6-0 v Bristol City Division 3(S) Dec 27 1932 Bourton (3), Lake (2), White.

6-0 v Torquay Utd Division 3(S) Nov 3 1934 Bourton (2), Lake (2), Jones, Birtley.

6-0 v Newport County Division 2 Jan 18 1947 Lowrie (3), Roberts (2), Ashall.

6-0 v Swindon Town Division 3(S). Oct. 1, 1955 Scorers: Hawkings (3), Sambrook (2), Harvey.

6-0 v Aldershot Division 3(S) Mar 17 1958. Scorers: Rogers (3), Hill P. (3).

7-2 v Torquay Utd Division 3(S) Dec 13 1952. Scorers: Dorman (3), Brown (3), Waldock.

BIGGEST CUP WINS HOME (1919 onwards):

8-0 v Rushden & Diamonds League Cup R2 Oct 2, 2002. Scorers: McSheffrey (3), Mills (2), Bothroyd (2), Betts (p).

CYRILLE REGIS
COVENTRY CITY

Cyrille Regis hit five in City's 7-2 win over Chester in 1985

7-0 v Scunthorpe Utd FA Cup R1. Nov. 24 1934. Scorers: Birtley (2), Lauderdale (2), Bourton, Jones, Liddle.

7-0 v Macclesfield Town FA Cup R3. Jan 2 1999. Scorers: Huckerby (3), Boateng, Whelan, Froggatt, o.g.

7-1 v Bath City FA Cup R2. Dec 14 1929. Scorers: Loughlin (2), Lake (2), Widdowson, Pick, Dugdale.

7-2 v Chester City League Cup R2 Oct. 9, 1985. Scorers: Regis (5), Gibson, Kilcline.

5-0 v Watford. League Cup R5 R Dec 9 1980. Scorers: Hateley (2), Bodak, Thompson, Hunt.

5-0 v Sunderland League Cup R5 R Jan 24, 1990. Scorers: Livingstone (4), Gynn.

5-1 v Darlington League Cup R2 Oct 8 1973. Scorers: Stein (3), Coop, Green.

4-0 v Scunthorpe Utd FA Cup R2 Dec 11 1954. Scorers: Capel (2), Harvey, Lee.

4-0 v Oxford Utd FA Cup R5 Feb 13, 1982 Scorers: Thompson (2), Hunt (2).

4-0 v Rochdale League Cup R2 (1st leg) Sep 25 1991. Scorers: Rosario (2), Gallacher, McGrath.

5-2 v Newport County FA Cup R3. Jan 11 1947. Scorers: Lowrie (3), Roberts, Ashall.

BIGGEST LEAGUE WINS AWAY (1919 onwards):

7-0 v Aberdare A Division 3(S) Apr 18 1927. Scorers: Heathcote (2), McClure, Crisp, Bird, Herbert, Ferguson.

6-1 v Carlisle Utd Division 4 Feb 14 1959 Scorers: Stewart (4), Straw, Daley.

6-1 v Crewe Alex Division 1 Feb. 9 2002. Scorers: Hughes (3), Delorge (2), Thompson.

6-1 v Walsall Division 1 Jan 17 2004 Scorers: Morrell (2), McSheffrey (2), Joachim, o.g.

5-1 v QPR. Division 3(S) Apr 26 1928. Scorers: Dinsdale (3), Ramage P. (2).

5-1 v Bolton W. Premiership. Jan. 31, 1998. Scorers: Huckerby (2), Dublin (2), Whelan.

4-0 v Bury Division 2 Jan. 2 1936. Scorers: Brown (2), Lake, Liddle.

4-0 v Southampton Division 2 Apr 16 1937. Scorers: Lager (2), Roberts, Taylor.

4-0 v Newcastle Utd Division 2 Feb. 4 1938. Scorers: Crawley (2), Davidson, Taylor.

4-0 v Brentford Division 2 Oct. 7 1950 Scorers: Simpson, Allen, Chisholm, Lockhart.

7-3 v Gillingham Division 3(S) Dec 30 1933 Scorers: Bacon (5), Lake, White.

6-3 v QPR Division 3 Nov 30 1963 Scorers: Hudson (3), Hale, Rees, Humphries.

BIGGEST CUP WINS AWAY (1919 onwards):

6-1 v Trowbridge FA Cup R1 Nov. 16 1963. Scorers: Hudson (3), Rees, Kearns, o.g.

5-1 v Lincoln City FA Cup R3 Mar 7 1963 Whitehouse, Bly, Barr, Farmer, og.

4-0 v Hartlepools U FA Cup R2 Dec 8 1934 Bourton (2), Jones, Birtley.

4-0 v Bournemouth League Cup R2 Sep 27 1988 Gynn (2), Downs, Bannister.

4-0 v Southend U League Cup R2 Sep 22 1998 Boateng, Dublin, Whelan, Soltvedt.

5-2 v Weymouth FA Cup R1 Nov 16 1958. Hill P (2), Straw (2), Boxley.

4-1 v Bishop Auckland FA Cup R2 Dec6 1952. Dorman, Waldock, Johnson, og.

4-1 v Worcester C FA Cup R1 Nov 5 1960. Farmer (2), Myerscough (2).

4-1 v Orient FA Cup R3 Jan 13 1973. Alderson (2), Carr, Hutchison.

WINSTON CHURCHILL TROPHY

When Winston Churchill died on January 24, 1965, the trophy was inaugurated by Chairman Derrick Robins with both teams out of the FA Cup and a gap in the fixtures on the day of the funeral, Saturday January 30th.

v Fulham (h) Jan 30 1965. Att. 10,881. Result L 1-2. Scorer: Hudson. *Fulham won the trophy which looked suspiciously like the FA Cup. George Cohen and Johnny Haynes scored for Fulham.*

v Northampton Town (h) May 10 1966. Att. 13,576. Result D 2-2. Scorers: Denton, Pointer. *Match combined as testimonial for George Curtis and Mick Kearns. Former Sky Blues hero George Hudson returned just a couple of months after his shock transfer to Northampton, but failed to score for the Cobblers.*

v West Ham United (h) Mar. 3 1967. Att. 18,524. Result D 3-3. Scorers: Gibson, Machin (2). *West Ham won the cup on penalties, their second victory in the Challenge. With ten minutes to go and the scores equal, the crowd whistled for an end, in order to witness the unusual event at the time, of a penalty shoot-out.*

WOOD, ALF

Alf Wood, at 43 was the oldest player ever to play for Coventry City player and one of the longest serving men in the club's history.

Born in Aldridge, Staffordshire on May 14, 1915 he played for Nuneaton and Sutton Town before joining Coventry City in December 1935. He made two appearances prior to the war. During World War Two he played for the Army and made guest appearances for Northampton Town.

Towards the end of the war he contracted meningitis and was told by doctors that he would not play football again. Wood defied the medical prognosis and went on to make 209 consecutive appearances for the club between 1946-51. Alf was regarded by Bob Dennison, Coventry chief scout in the 1970s, as the best uncapped English goalkeeper in his heyday.

After ten games of the 1951-52 season Wood was dropped in favour of Peter Taylor. In December 1951 he moved on to Northampton Town for a £2,100 transfer fee. Wood played against City in 1954 when he helpfully let in a freak goal from Roy Kirk, the only goal of the game.

Clearly a Coventry man through and through, Alf returned to Highfield Road as assistant trainer in the summer of 1955. He served under managers Jesse Carver, George Raynor and Billy Frith.

Having retired from playing and by now working on the coaching staff, Wood shocked the football world when he stepped in for the injured Jim Sanders during the 1958-59 season. He kept four clean sheets during his return spell and even saved a penalty in a 2-0 win over York City.

Alf made the last of 12 appearances in an FA Cup tie against Plymouth Argyle on December 7, 1958, more than twenty years after his debut. He continued as trainer with the club until he lost his job in 1961 when there was a wholesale clearout of backroom staff after the appointment of Jimmy Hill as manager.

Sacked in November 1961, he was out of football until he was appointed as Walsall coach in October 1963 and a month later became manager of the Saddlers. He left in October 1964, but by then had discovered Allan Clarke, the striker who went on to play for Fulham, Leicester City, Leeds United and England.

Wood returned to Coventry in semi-retirement to manage the Massey Ferguson works football team.

Over his two spells at Highfield Road, Alf Wood was with Coventry City for some 20 years. Despite his loyal service to the club he was never granted a testimonial. He died in 2001.
Player 1937-51 & 1956-58. 246 apps. Trainer/Coach 1955-61.

WORLD CUP
George Raynor, City manager in 1956, had previously been coach of the Sweden team that reached third place in the World Cup in 1950, in Brazil.

After his brief time at Coventry, he returned to Sweden and became national manager for the second time. Clearly at home there, Raynor led the Swedish team to the runners-up spot in the 1958 World Cup. Sweden, the hosts, lost to Brazil in the final 2-5 in Stockholm. (see: Olympics)

***

The first Coventry City player to be sent off in a World Cup match was Nii Lamptey playing for Ghana.

***

The fastest recorded sending off in the World Cup was 55 seconds when Uruguayan player Batista fouled Gordon Strachan of Scotland in Mexico in 1986.

***

John Aloisi of Coventry City scored a double hat-trick for Australia in one World Cup qualifying match. His six goals at Coffs Harbour, New South Wales, on April 9, 2001, contributed to the Socceroos beating Tonga 22-0.

The scoreline was the greatest ever international victory, eclipsing Iran's 19-0 win over Guam.

However, two days later it was made to look like a close fought contest when the Aussies beat American Samoa 31-0. This time though, Aloisi did not play.

MAS DAY

Never mind talk of a winter break! At Coventry we say, *"Bring back Christmas Day Games!"*

Christmas Day was on the fixture list 25 times between 1919 and 1959. City's impressive record in Football League games on Xmas Day is: P25 W16 D2 L7

***

During the period that league football was played on Christmas Day, it was traditional to play two games in two days against the *same* opponents, the reverse fixture often being on December 26th. Boxing Day/St.Stephens Day) followed the Christmas day game in the following years: 1919; 1922; 1923; 1925; 1928; 1929; 1930; 1931; 1933;

1934; 1935; 1936; 1946; 1947; 1950; 1951; 1953; 1957; 1959.

***

Coventry City's Biggest Win on Christmas Day:
7-1 v Wolverhampton W. (h) Division 2. 1922.
Scorers: Tomms (3), Richmond (2), Jones, Wood.
Other Big Christmas Day Wins:
5-1 v Sheffield Wednesday (h) 1923
5-1 v Reading (h) 1931
4-1 v Cardiff City (h) 1933
4-0 v Gillingham (h) 1934
5-3 v Wrexham (h) 1959*
The last time Coventry played on Christmas Day.

***

Biggest Christmas Day Attendance:
Home: 32,042 v Southampton 1936. Result W 2-0.
Away: 49,019 v Sheffield United 1937. Result L 2-3.

***

Coventry's first Christmas Day League win was in 1919. It was also their first win that 1919-20 season. They beat Stoke City 3-2 in a home morning game in front of 19,000 spectators.

***

Goalkeeper Jerry Best made his debut on Christmas Day 1920 against Cardiff City in a 2-4 defeat.

***

Coventry players Harry Barratt, Paul Edwards and Gary McAllister were born on Christmas Day.

***

Despite their Christian names, Noel Simpson, Noel

John Aloisi

Cantwell and Noel Whelan were *not* born on Christmas Day.

X-PLETIVES

It's enough to make you swear, watching Coventry Cityas at least one media pundits can testify.

Malcolm Allison, former manager of Manchester City and Middlesbrough was working as a pundit for Century Radio in the North East in 1996.

When the Middlesbrough goalie Gary Walsh let in a weak shot from Les Ferdinand, his expert contribution to the listeners' understanding of the game was, "F***ing Hell!" He was duly sacked only to be forgiven and return for the 1996-97 season as resident pundit for the Boro fans. However, on December 28th, with the Sky Blues storming into a 3-0 lead over Middlesbrough, Allison was live and dangerous again, using the F-word in frustration. This time the boot was permanent.

Colin Stein

Former Coventry striker **Colin Stein** was instrumental in getting one local radio reporter temporarily removed from the airways in the late 1970s. The hapless hack in question was commentating on Stein's club Rangers when the striker was presented with a golden opportunity. "Stein must score!" he exclaimed and when, inexplicably, Stein didn't he rashly added: "F*** me, he's missed it!"

YET TO MEET IN THE LEAGUE

Coventry City have not yet played Football League games against these clubs:
Barnet
Boston United
Cheltenham Town
Macclesfield Town*
Rushden and Diamonds*
Scunthorpe United*
Wycombe Wanderers*
Yeovil Town

City also never played league games against the following clubs, during their terms in the Football League:
Cambridge United*
Hereford United
Kidderminster Harriers
Maidstone United
Scarborough*
*City have played cup ties against these teams.

YOUNGEST GOALKEEPER

Perry Suckling. 16 years 320 days. v. Southampton (h) W 1-0. August 28, 1982.

YOUNGEST INTERNATIONAL

Jimmy Holmes made his debut for Ireland against Austria on May 30, 1971, before his first Coventry City appearance. He is the Republic's youngest international player at 17 years, 200 days of age. Holmes made his debut for the Sky Blues some five months later against Leicester City on December 4, 1971.

YOUNGEST MANAGER

Terry Butcher. 31 years 11 months. Appointed November 1990.

YOUNGEST PLAYERS

The youngest players ever to make a first-team appearance for Coventry City are

1 **Ben Mackey**   Apr 12 2003   16 years 167 days
Ipswich Town (h) L 2-4 *sub.*
2 **Gary McSheffrey**   Feb 27 1999   16 years 198 days
Aston Villa (a) W 4-1 *sub.*
3 **Brian Hill**   Apr 30 1958   16 years 273 days
Gillingham (a) L 2-3 *scored*
4 **Isaac Osbourne**   Apr 26 2003   16 years 308 days
Gillingham (h) D 0-0
5 **Perry Suckling**   Aug 28 1982   16 years 320 days
Southampton (h) W 1-0 *goalie*
6 **George Curtis**   Apr 21 1956   16 years 351 days
Newport County (a) L 2-4
7 **Dietmar Bruck**   Apr 281961   17 years   9 days
Swindon Town (h) D 1-1
8 **Colin Holder**   Mar 20 1961   17 years   73 days
Newport County (a) D 3-3
9 **Lol Harvey**   Nov 3 1951   17 years 101 days
Brentford (a) L 0-1
10 **Bobby Parker**   Mar 28 1970   17 years 137 days
Burnley (h) D 1-1
11 **Bobby Gould**   Oct 30 1964   17 years 140 days
Shrewsbury Town (a) D 0-0
12 **Keith Thompson** Sep 18 1982   17 years 147 days
Birmingham City (a) D 0-0
13 **Tom Bates**   Apr 5 2003   17 years 156 days
Preston North End (a) D 2-2 *sub.*

ZERO

The number of times Coventry City have finished in the top six of any division in the 35 years between 1970 and 2005. City are the only club not to achieve a top six in that time.

APPENDIX

ATTENDANCES
HIGHEST ATTENDANCES NEUTRAL VENUE
98,000 v Tottenham Hotspur FA Cup Final Wembley May 16 1987 W 3-2
88,000 v Everton Charity Shield Wembley Aug 1 1987 L 0-1
51,372 v Leeds Utd FA Cup Semi-Final Hillsborough Sheffield Apr 12 1987 W 3-2
15,867 v Portsmouth FA Cup R4 (2nd rep) White Hart Lane London Mar 19 1963 W 2-1
 8,113 v Luton Town League Cup R3 Filbert Street Leicester Oct 27 1987 L 1-3
 6,756 v Reading FA Cup R2 (2nd rep) Stamford Bridge London Dec 19 1932 L 0-1
 2,000 v Carlisle U FA Cup Prem R (2nd rep) Hyde Road Manchester Dec14 1908 L 1-3 (aet)*
* This match was only settled after a second period of extra time The 150 minute match is the longest in the club's history.
These are the only matches that Coventry City has played at a neutral ground in full competition.

HIGHEST ATTENDANCES HOME – LEAGUE
The following includes statistics from 1919 (when Coventry City became a league club) but does not include statistics from World War Two (1939-46) Coventry City score appears first.
51,455 v Wolverhampton W Div 2 Apr 29 1967 W 3-1
47,111 v Manchester Utd Div 1 Mar 16 1968 W 2-0
45,402 v Manchester Utd Div 1 Apr 8 1969 W 2-1
44,930 v Aston Villa Div 2 Mar 12 1938 L 0-1
43,446 v Manchester Utd Div 1 Nov 8 1969 L 1-2
42,975 v Luton Town* Div 3(S) Apr 27 1936 0-0
42,911 v Manchester Utd Div 1 Jan 27 1973 1-1
42,207 v Liverpool Div 1 Dec 26 1967 1-1
41,846 v Leicester City Div 1 Apr 1 1969 W 1-0
41,212 v Nottingham F Div 1 Aug 29 1967 W 1-3
41,036 v Derby County Div 1 Aug 16 1969 1-1
40,950 v Tottenham H Div 1 Sep 17 1968 L 1-2
40,718 v Sheffield Utd Div 2 Dec 27 1937 2-2

40,022 v Leeds Utd Div 1 Feb 26 1971 L 0-1
*The official attendance of this game does not allow for a good many gatecrashers. Even so it is more than attended the Arsenal v Chelsea London derby on the same day which was watched by 40,402.

●The all-time best attendance for a reserve match at Highfield Road is 12,132 in April 1965 for a match against QPR reserves Another big crowd was recorded when 10,302 attended the Central League game between City reserves and Manchester Utd reserves in August 1968.

●Attendances of 10,295 and 15,329 were registered for live close-circuit televised games at Highfield Road when the Sky Blues were away at Cardiff City and Charlton Athletic in the 1965-66 season.

HIGHEST ATTENDANCES HOME – CUPS
44,492 v West Brom FA Cup R5 Feb 20 1937 L 2-3
44,000 v Manchester Utd FA Cup R6 Mar 30 1963 L 1-3
41,281 v Derby County FA Cup R4 Jan 27 1974 D 0-0
40,487 v Sunderland** FA Cup R5 Mar 25 1963 W 2-1
38,814 v Grimsby Town FA Cup R4 Feb 3 1973 W 1-0
38,476 v West Brom League Cup R4 Nov 3 1965 D 1-1
38,046 v West Brom FA Cup R3 Jan 9 1979 D 2-2
36,105 v Liverpool League Cup R4 R Dec 20 1977 L 0-2
35,569 v Newcastle Utd FA Cup R3 Jan 28 1967 L 3-4
35,468 v West Ham League Cup SF Jan 27 1981 W 3-2
34,278 v Walsall FA Cup R3 Jan 10 1948 W 2-1
32,831 v Tranmere FA Cup R4 Feb 17 1968 D 1-1
31,724 v Hull City FA Cup R5 Feb 24 1973 W 3-0
31,673 v Sunderland FA Cup R3 Jan 11 1930 L 1-2
**Eyewitnesses estimate an unofficial attendance of 47-48,000 including gatecrashers

HIGHEST ATTENDANCES AWAY – LEAGUE
68,029 v Aston Villa Div 2 Oct 30 1937 D 1-1
67,637 v Manchester Utd Premier Apr 14 2001 L 2-4
63,686 v Aston Villa Division 2 Oct 3 1936 D 0-0
61,380 v Manchester Utd Premier Feb 5 2000 L 2-3
55,726 v Manchester Utd Division 1 Aug 24 1977 L 1-2

55,569 v Newcastle Utd Division 2 Oct 4 1947 D 0-0
55,313 v Newcastle Utd Division 2 Sep 11 1946 L 1-3
55,230 v Manchester Utd Premier Mar 1 1997 L 1-3
55,193 v Manchester Utd Premier Sep 12 1998 L 0-2
55,074 v Manchester Utd Premier Aug 30 1997 L 0-3
54,375 v Tottenham H Division 2 Oct 15 1949 L 1-3
54,253 v Manchester Utd Division 1 Oct 25 1967 L 0-4
52,169 v Manchester Utd Division 1 Aug 27 1975 D 1-1

HIGHEST ATTENDANCES AWAY – CUPS
60,350 v Everton FA Cup R5 Mar 5 1966 L 0-3
53,289 v Everton FA Cup R4 Jan 25 1969 L 0-2
51,261 v Liverpool FA Cup R3 R Jan 12 1970 L 0-3
50,106 v Wolverhampton FA Cup R6 Mar 17 1973 L 0-2
49,082 v Manchester Utd FA Cup R4 Jan 31 1987 W 1-0
48,005 v Sheffield Wed FA Cup R6 Mar 14 1987 W 3-1
47,656 v Aston Villa FA Cup R3 Jan 9 1965 L 0-3
44,676 v Newcastle FA Cup R4 (rep) Jan 28 1976 L 0-5
41,078 v Arsenal FA Cup R4 Jan 29 1977 L 1-3
41,056 v Burnley FA Cup R4 Feb 2 1952 L 0-2
40,349 v Birmingham FA Cup R3 Jan 12 1935 L 1-5
39,790 v Burnley FA Cup R4 Jan 25 1947 L 0-2
38,039 v Manchester Utd FA Cup R4 Jan 26 1985 L 1-2
36,988 v Sunderland FA Cup R3 Jan 6 1951 L 0-2
36,979 v Aston Villa FA Cup R5 Feb 14 1998 W 1-0
36,688 v Tottenham H FA Cup R5 Feb 14 1981 L 1-3
36,551 v West Ham League Cup SF Feb 10 1981 L 0-2
36,262 v West Brom FA Cup R3 (rep) Jan 15 1979 L 0-4
36,116 v Leicester City FA Cup R3 Jan 12 1952 D 1-1

LOWEST ATTENDANCES HOME – LEAGUE
1,660 v Hartlepools Utd Division 3(N) Apr 24 1926 W5-2
2,059 v Crystal Palace Division 3(S) Feb 13 1928 D 2-2
3,000 v Portsmouth Division 2 Feb 12 1925 W 2-1
3,936 v Newport CountyDivision 3(S) Apr 4 1955 W 3-2
4,000 v Fulham Division 2 Dec 11 1922 W 1-0
4,785 v Queens Park R Division 3(S) Apr 1954 W 3-1
5,000 v Tranmere Division 3(N) Mar 27 1926 L 1-2
5,000 v Chesterfield Division 3(N) Apr 10 1926 L 2-4
5,000 v Luton Town Division 3(S) Nov 13 1926 W 4-1
5,000 v Queens Park R Division 3(S) Dec 27 1927 D0-0
5,000 v Bournemouth Division 3(S) Mar 10 1928 W 3-2
5,329 v Brighton & HA Division 3(S) Apr 18 1931 D 0-0

5,517 v Crystal Palace Division 3(S) Apr 1 1957 D 3-3
5,569 v Newport County Division 3(S) Apr 8 1957 W 2-0
5,830 v Aldershot Division 3(S) Mar 17 1958 W 6-0
5,894 v Port Vale Division 3 Apr 16 1962 L 0-1
5,965 v Bristol City Division 3 Apr 23 1962 D 1-1
6,914 v Gillingham Division 3(S) Apr 26 1958 D 1-1
7,142 v Bradford CityDivision 3 Oct 9 1961 W 3-0
7,233 v Watford Division 3 Mar 12 1962 W 1-0
7,412 v Southend Utd Division 3 Oct 8 1960 W 3-0
7,478 v Watford Division 1 Jan 18 1986 L 0-2
7,532 v Norwich City Division 3(S) Apr 21 1958 W 2-1
7,573 v Hull City Division 3 Apr 28 1962 L 0-2

LOWEST ATTENDANCES HOME – CUPS
5,519 v Chester City League Cup R2 Oct 9 1985 W 7-2
5,980 v Rochdale League Cup R2 Sep 25 1991 W 4-0
5,989 v Scarborough League Cup R2 Sep 23 1992 W2-0
6,075 v Colchester League Cup R1 Sep 11 2002 W 3-0
6,146 v Bolton League Cup R2 Sep 26 1990 W 4-2
6,180 v Torquay League Cup R1 Aug 25 2004 W 4-1
6,573 v Rotherham League Cup R2 Sep 23 1986 W 3-2
6,631 v Southend League Cup R2 Sep 16 1998 W 1-0
6,643 v Barrow League Cup R1 Oct 10 1960 W 4-2
7,212 v Bournemouth League Cup R2 Oct 11 1988 W 3-1
7,425 v Preston League Cup R2 Sep 27 2000 W 4-1
7,437 v Burnley League Cup R3 Nov 9 1982 L 1-2
7,629 v Crewe Alexandra FA Cup R3 Jan 8 2005 W 3-0
7,698 v Hull City League Cup R3 Oct 31 1990 W 3-0
7,702 v Norwich City FA Cup R1 R Dec 4 1929 W 2-0
8,000 v Rotherham County FA Cup QR5 R Dec 8 1921 W 1-0
8,249 v Fulham League Cup R2 Oct 26 1982 D 0-0
8,280 v Peterborough League Cup R1 Aug 13 2003 W2-0
8,579 v Rushden & D League Cup R2 Oct 2 2002 W8-0
8,583 v Oldham League Cup R3 Oct 28 1986 W 2-1
8,615 v Wrexham League Cup R2 Oct 5 1994 W 3-2
8,633 v Exeter City FA Cup R2 R Dec 18 1930 L 1-2
8,652 v Grimsby T League Cup R2 Oct 25 1983 W 2-1
8,769 v Darlington League Cup R2 Oct 8 1973 W 5-1
8,772 v Hartlepool League Cup R2 Sep 5 1972 W 1-0
8,915 v Hull City League Cup R2 Sep 20 1995 W 2-0
9,000 v Tranmere FA Cup QR5 Dec 1 1923 D 2-2
9,197 v Walsall League Cup R2 Oct 9 1984 L 0-3
9,605 v Blackpool League Cup R2 Oct 1 1997 W 3-1

9,656 v Wycombe League Cup R2 Sep 22 1993 W 3-0
9,814 v West Brom League Cup R3 Oct 29 1985 D 0-0

LOWEST ATTENDANCES AWAY – LEAGUE

Also known as the "You must have come in a taxi" section

  683 v Merthyr Town Division 3(S) Apr 14 1930 D 2-2
1,058 v Thames Division 3(S) Jan 17 1931 W 2-1
1,215 v Thames Division 3(S) Jan 16 1932 L 2-5
2,000 v Hartlepools Utd Division 3(N) Dec 12 1925 L 2-3
2,077 v Wimbledon Division 1 Sep 21 2002 W 1-0
2,275 v Southport Division 4 Apr 13 1959 W 2-1
2,351 v Halifax Town Division 3 Apr 30 1962 W 2-0
2,500 v Merthyr Town Division 3(S) Sep 24 1927 L 2-3
2,505 v Clapton Orient Division 3(S) Jan 16 1936 W 1-0
2,681 v Northampton T Division 3(S) Feb 25 1933 L 1-5
2,862 v Crystal Palace Division 3(S) Nov 9 1929 L 3-4
2,950 v Newport County Division 3(S) Mar 28 1931 D 1-1
3,000 v Merthyr Town Division 3(S) Feb 2 1929 D 2-2
3,000 v Bristol Rovers Division 3(S) May 6 1933 L 0-1
3,060 v Brighton & HA Division 3(S) Apr 22 1931 L 0-2
3,146 v Torquay Utd Division 3(S) Nov 18 1933 W 3-1
3,234 v Swindon Town Division 3(S) May 1 1935 D 0-0
3,245 v Queens Park R Division 3 May 24 1963 W 3-1
3,270 v Wimbledon Division 1 Dec 28 1991 D 1-1
3,360 v Newport County Division 3 Dec 23 1961 W 2-1
3,379 v Torquay Utd Division 3 Feb 24 1962 L 0-1
3,384 v Brighton & HA Division 3(S) May 7 1955 L 0-2
3,477 v Swindon Town Division 3(S) Feb 11 1933 W 2-1
3,500 v Torquay Utd Division 3(S) Apr 7 1928 W 3-2
3,500 v Swindon Town Division 3(S) Sep 17 1930 L 0-4
3,593 v Torquay Utd Division 3(S) Mar 16 1935 L 0-1
3,660 v Newport County Division 3 Mar 20 1961 D 3-3
3,742 v Halifax Town Division 3 Nov 17 1962 W 4-2
3,759 v Wimbledon Premier Aug 22 1992 W 2-1
3,797 v Aberdare Athletic Division 3(S) Apr 18 1927 W 7-0
3,817 v Hull City Division 3 Dec 9 1961 L 1-3
3,925 v Aldershot Division 4 Oct 1 1958 W 4-1

●The demolition of the gasworks on the site of the new stadium in September 2002 is thought to have attracted a bigger crowd than the 2,077 in the away game against Wimbledon in the same week.

LOWEST ATTENDANCES AWAY – CUPS

2,288 v Rochdale   League Cup R2 Oct 8 1991 L 0-1
2,633 v Scarborough League Cup R2 Oct 7 1992 L 0-3
3,500 v Clapton Orient FA Cup R1 R Dec 2 1932 L 0-2
3,821 v Luton Town League Cup R1 Sep 25 1963 W 4-3
4,410 v Worksop FA Cup R1 Nov 28 1925 L 0-1
4,523 v Portsmouth League Cup R2 Nov 2 1961 L 0-2
4,682 v Workington T League Cup R1 Sep 13 1961 L 0-3
4,694 v Rotherham U League Cup R2 Oct 7 1986 W 1-0
4,741 v Guildford FA Cup R1 Nov 26 1932 W 2-1
5,166 v Cambridge U League Cup R2 Sep 22 1987 W 1-0
5,222 v Bolton League Cup R2 Oct 9 1990 W 3-2
5,286 v Wrexham League Cup R2 Sep 20 1994 W 2-1
5,326 v Leyton Orient League Cup R2 Sep 22 1965 W 3-0
5,530 v Colchester U FA Cup R4 Feb 3 2004 L 1-3
5,729 v Peterborough League Cup R2 Sep 11 2001 D 2-2
5,884 v Blackpool League Cup R2 Sep 16 1997 L 0-1
5,993 v Wycombe W League Cup R2 Oct 5 1993 L 2-4
6,000 v Woking FA Cup R3 (rep) Feb 4 1997 W 2-1
6,088 v Grimsby Town League Cup R2 Oct 4 1983 D 0-0
6,200 v Aldershot FA Cup R2 Dec 7 1957 L 1-4
6,237 v Fulham League Cup R2 Oct 5 1982 D 2-2
6,292 v Southend League Cup R2 Sep 22 1998 W 4-0
6,453 v Bournemouth League Cup R2 Sep 27 1988 W 4-0
6,524 v Trowbridge   FA Cup R1 Nov 16 1963 W 6-1
6,759 v Tranmere League Cup R2 Sep 14 1999 L 1-5
6,929 v Hull City League Cup R2 Oct 4 1995 W 1-0

OTHER LOW ATTENDANCES

Matches pre-1919 or in optional cups
1,086 v Millwall (h) Full Members Cup Oct 15 1985 D 1-1
2,000 v Walsall (h) FA Cup QR2 Oct 15 1904 W 2-0
2,000 v Brierley Hill (a) FA Cup QR1 Sep 21 1907 W 6-2
2,000 v Oswestry U (a) FA Cup QR5 Nov 23 1907 D 2-2
2,000 v Stafford Rangers (a) FA Cup QR3 Oct 29 1904 L 2-3
3,000 v Kettering (a) FA Cup QR5 Dec 4 1909 W 5-0
3,000 v Bilston (h) FA Cup QR3 Oct 26 1907 W 2-1
3,516 v Stoke City (a) Full Members Cup Sep 18 1985 L 0-3
3,781 v Wimbledon (h) Zenith Data Systems Cup Nov 29 1989 L 1-3 (aet)
4,000 v Darlaston (h) FA Cup QR2 Oct 5 1907 W 7-1
4,259 v Worcester City (h) FA Cup QR4 Nov 2 1907 W 2-0
5,000 v Carlisle Utd (a) FA Cup PR(rep) Dec 10 1908 D 1-1

5,000 v Walsall (h) FA Cup QR1 Oct 31 1903 L 2-4
6,215 v Carlisle Utd (h) FA Cup PR Dec 5 1908 D 1-1
7,000 v Wrexham (h) FA Cup QR4 Nov 20 1909 W 3-0

FRIENDLIES, AWAY
MID-SEASON AWAY FRIENDLIES

v Reading Dec 12 1953 Att 3,115 D 0-0. *An early example of a mid-season friendly of questionable merit.*

v Bristol Rovers Feb 17 1962 Att 4,533 D 1-1. Scorer: McCann. *Coventry play three friendlies in a week. This away game was sandwiched by two at home See: Friendlies at Highfield Road – Mid Season.*

v Linfield Nov 14 1962 W 2-1. Scorers: Hill B, Whitehouse. *City fly to Belfast for a mid-season away benefit friendly against Hugh Barr's old team at Windsor Park.*

v Manchester Utd Feb 2 1963 Att 15,000 D 2-2. Scorers: Farmer, Whitehouse. Friendly match during the winter "Big Freeze" Played at Shamrock Rovers' Glenmaiure Park Dublin This was City's first match of any sort since Dec 28th 1962.

v Wolverhampton W Feb 9 1963 Att 6,500 L 0-3. *Friendly match during "Big Freeze". Played at Cork Hibernians' Flower Lodge Ground Terry Bly suffered from air sickness on the journey and withdrew from the game.*

v Wolverhampton W Feb 20 1963 Att 6,000 L 3-6. Scorers: Hale (2), Hill B. *A third game in Ireland to escape the winter "Big Freeze and the fourth trip to the emerald isle this season" Played at Linfield's ground Belfast.*

v Greenock Morton Mar 24 1965 Att 4,000 L 1-3 (L 3-5 on agg). Scorer: Clements. *"Enterprise Cup" 2nd Leg Played in a snowstorm. The Cup was originated when newspapers nominated Morton and Coventry as the most enterprising clubs in British football See: Friendlies at Highfield Road for details of 1st leg.*

v Ashford Town Oct 17 1966 Att 1,200. W 11-0 Scorers: Farmer, Gould (3), Tudor (2), Key (2), Curtis, Mitten, Hill B. *City travel to Kent to get some shooting practice.*

v Torquay Utd Nov 3 1969 Att 5,796 W 2-1 Scorer: Joicey (2).

v Northampton T Nov 10 1969 Att 2,955. W 2-1 Scorers: Hunt, McMahon. *These two friendlies in November seem to do the trick as the team goes on to win five league games in a row.*

v Luton Town Jan 23 1971 Att 7,154 W 2-1 Scorers: Rafferty, og. *Knocked out of the FA Cup (to Rochdale) this friendly gives first team experience to youngsters Mick McGuire Billy Rafferty and Jimmy Holmes.*

v Bournemouth Mar 3 1971 Att 4,459 W 1-0 Scorer: Alderson.

v Torquay Utd Oct 25 1971 Att 2,002 L 1-4 Scorer: Carr.

v Norwich City Feb 26 1972 Att 11,615 L 1-2 Scorer: Young.

v The British Army Oct 8th 1974 W 4-0 Scorers: Cartwright (2), Green, McGuire. *At Aldershot to inaugurate the new floodlights at the Military Stadium*

v Newport County Dec 1 1976 Att 2,997 W 7-1 Scorers: Wallace (3), Ferguson, Powell, McDonald, Murphy. *A mid-season friendly which helps the strikers to find their scoring touch.*

v Banbury Utd Apr 25 1979 Att 2,000 W 3-0 Scorers: Hutchison, McDonald, Bannister. *Benefit Match for club in financial hardship.*

v Hastings Utd Dec 17 1980 Att 1,066 W 2-1 Scorers: Bannister Whitton. *Friendly to mark the switch-on of the Sussex club's new floodlights City win the battle.*

v Nuneaton Borough Mar 7 1983 Att 4,317 L 1-2 Scorer: Dyson. *Mid-season away friendly George Best was guest player for Nuneaton and scored one of the Boro' goals with a penalty. City played the first half with three defenders in attack and three strikers in defence.*

v St Albans Sep 4 1995 W 7-1 Scorers: Ndlovu (3), Strachan, Lamptey, og (2). *An unusual friendly only a few weeks into the season Nii Lamptey's first game for the club. Ndlovu scored his second hat-trick in consecutive friendlies following a pre-season one against Aberdeen.*

v Jersey Nov 10 1996 W 10-1 Scorers: Whelan (3), Huckerby (2), O'Neill, Shaw, McMenamin, Dublin, Telfer. *Mid-season away friendly at Springfield Stadium St Hellier against the National Squad of the Channel Island. Darren Huckerby, then on-loan from Newcastle, made an outstanding contribution.*

END-OF-SEASON AWAY FRIENDLIES

v Dublin XI Apr 27 1964 Att 5,000 W 3-4 Scorers: Hudson, Barr, Farmer. *At Dalymount Park home of Bohemians. This match was the first of the "Five in Five" that City played to celebrate winning the Division Three Championship. The five games in five days included the Bedworth and Eastbourne games (below) (for the two home games. See: Friendlies at Highfield Road End-of-Season.*

v Bedworth Utd Apr 29 1964 Att 4,500 W 4-0 Scorers: Newton Bruck, Tedds, Rees. *Match three of the "Five in Five" sequence. See: Friendlies at Highfield Road End-of-Season.*

v Eastbourne May 1 1964 Att 1,000 W 3-1 Scorers: Kirby (2), Hudson. *The fifth of the "Five in Five" games and the Sky Blues' sixth match in seven days. Manager Jimmy Hill played It is believed to be the only time he played for Coventry City The match receipts were for charity (see: Friendlies at Highfield Road End-of-Season).*

v Bedworth Utd May 12 1966 Att 2,000 W 4-3 Scorers: Farmer, Bruck, Pointer, Burkitt. *Coventry's third game in three days Benefit game for the home club's floodlight appeal Bedworth's invitation XI included City reserve goalie Bob Wesson. The end of season atmosphere allowed Bill Glazier Sky Blues keeper to come upfield and join in play. When City were awarded a penalty George Curtis took a 70 yard run up only to have his shot saved. See: Winston Churchill Trophy for match on May 10th home v Northampton Town. See: Testimonials Away for match on May 11th.*

v Shamrock Rovers May 17 1966 Att 8,000 W 2-0 Scorers: Roberts, Pointer. *Played at Dalymount Park Dublin. The match was in aid of Irish polio victims. John Key was a guest player prior to joining City from Fulham.*

v Heart of Midlothian Apr 24 1970 Att 5,554 D 0-0 *"Challenge Match" at Tynecastle Edinburgh. Played on the eve of the Scotland v England international in Glasgow - also a 0-0 draw.*

v Bangor City May 17 1971 Att 5,000 L 2-4 Scorers: Rafferty, O'Rourke. *A season without end as the Sky v*

Blues return from Tunisia for a visit to North Wales. Bangor included guest players Tony Book Shay Brennan and John Hughes. Coach Bill Asprey played for Coventry.

v Cambridge Utd May 8 1973 Att 2,000 W 2-1 Scorers: Smith, Ferguson. *An Oxbridge double as the Sky Blues follow a testimonial in Oxford with this game a day later. Played at Milton Road Cambridge City's ground.*

v Hereford Utd May 9 1973 W 2-0 Scorers: Mortimer, Green. *Hereford were celebrating the completion of their first year in the Football League. Coventry continue a busy week winning their third game in three days.*

v Stockport County May 11 1973 Att 2,510 L 0-2 *City's fourth match in five days Bobby Parker scored an own goal.*

v Gainsborough May 17 1973 D 0-0 *Coventry haven't noticed the season is over then fail to score against non-league opposition in a meaningless match. They have a game a week later in Sweden.*

v Gillingham May 3 1974 Att 5,900 W 3-0 Scorers: Stein (2), Alderson.

v Mansfield Town Apr 28 1975 Att 9,321 D 1-1 Scorer: Ferguson. *Mansfield were celebrating winning the Division 4 Championship.*

v Charlton Athletic May 2 1975 Att 3,340 W 1-0 Scorer: og.

v Reading Apr 27 1976 Att 3,500 W 4-0 Scorers: Green (2), Craven, Murphy.

v Lincoln City Apr 28 1976 Att 10,000 D 2-2 Scorers: Green, Cartwright. *Fourth Division Championship Presentation game for Lincoln. It's the Sky Blues' second away friendly in two days.*

INCLUDED: Matches here are either mid-season or end-of-season away friendlies only.

NOT INCLUDED: Pre-season away friendly matches It would take a whole book to list them all and they often feature reserve or B-sides.

FRIENDLIES AT HIGHFIELD ROAD
PRE-SEASON HOME FRIENDLIES

v Nottingham Forest Aug 14 1965 Att 13,493 W 4-3 Scorers: Hudson (4).

v Hibernian Aug 2 1969 Att 10,853 D 1-1 Scorer: Martin.

v Huddersfield Town Aug 6 1971 Att 5,136 L 1-2 Scorer: Joicey.

v Northampton Town Aug 13 1974 W 3-1 Scorers: Stein (2), Cross.

v Coventry Sporting Aug 17 1976 W 8-0 Scorers: Green, og, Murphy, Beck, Cross, Craven, Holmes (pen), Thompson.

v Northampton Town Aug 4 1977 W 2-1 Scorers: Ferguson, Hutchison.

v Japan Aug 14 1978 Att 5,000 W 2-0 Scorers: Yorath, Ferguson.

v Zimbabwe Aug 19 1983 W 2-0 Scorers: Withey, George. *Guest player Charlie George got the second goal.*

v Banik Ostrava (Czech) Aug 10 1990 Att 2,917 W 3-2 Scorers: Speedie, Dobson, McGrath. *Dobson's goal a long-range shot is considered one of the best ever scored at the ground.*

v Halesowen Town Aug 14 1990 Att 735 L 0-1.

v Benfica (Portugal) Aug 10 1996 Att 10,995 L 2-7 Scorers: Dublin Whelan.

v Feyenoord (Neth) Aug 3 1997 W 2-1 Scorers: Salako, Soltvedt. *Future Coventry player George Boateng scored for Feyenoord.*

v Espanyol (Spain) Aug 8 1998 Att 5,436 D 1-1 Scorer: Boateng. *New signing Robert Jarni was paraded to the fans before the game but he was sold to Real Madrid before playing any games for Coventry City.*

v Ajax (Netherlands) Aug 12 2000 Att 11,306 L 1-3 Scorer: Roussel.

v KAA Ghent (Belgium) Aug 4 2001 W 1-0 Scorer: Guerrero.

v Dundee Utd Jul 27 2002 Att 4,452 D 1-1 Scorer: Eustace. *Before the match Ernie Hunt & Willie Carr performed a re-enactment of the Donkey Kick goal.*

v Wolverhampton W Aug 2 2003 Att 6,822 W 2-1 Scorers: Adebola Davenport.

v Norwich City Jul 31 2004 Att 5,484 D 0-0.

MID-SEASON HOME FRIENDLIES

v Calgary Hillhurst (Canada) Nov 25 1911 W 4-3

Scorers: Turnbull (2), Bradley, Jones.

v Austria Wien (Austria) Dec 5 1935 Att 3,000 W 4-2 Scorers: Liddle (2) Lake, Watson.

v Galatasaray (Turkey) Sep 18 1950 Att 9,350 W 2-1 Scorers: Simpson, Evans.

v Queen of the South Oct 21 1953 Att 16,923 D 1-1 Scorer: Dorman. *Inaugural game for Highfield Road's new floodlights.*

v Wolverhampton W Oct 28 1953 Att 16,680 W1-0 Scorer: Jamieson (pen).

v East Fife Nov 11 1953 Att 12,644 D 2-2 Scorers: Brown, Kirk. *The third of three mid-season floodlit friendlies. Former manager Harry Storer who had left the club a week earlier paid at the turnstiles to watch the game. He explained the reason for paying the six shillings for a seat. "Football is my life and I wanted to see my team play." Storer had been invited to return to attend any game as a guest of the club but preferred to pay.*

v Hadjuk Split (Yugoslavia) Jan 27 1954 Att 4,214 L 2-3 Scorers: Bradbury Brown.

v Birmingham City Oct 5 1955 Att 6,823 D 2-2 Scorers: Hill P, Dutton. *First in a series of three midweek floodlit friendlies.*

v Burnley Oct 10 1955 Att 11,843 L 1-2 Scorer: Sambrook.

v Sheffield Utd Oct 17 1955 Att 6,051 L 2-3 Scorers: Uphill, Wyer.

v San Lorenzo (Argentina) Jan 30 1956 Att 17,357 *Abandoned after 43mins with the score 1-1.See Friendly Fiasco, Sky Blue Heaven Volume 1.*

v Burnley Oct 1 1956 Att 3,222 D 1-1 Scorer: McPherson. *Forty-year-old goalkeeper Alf Wood saved a penalty.*

v Nottingham Forest Oct 15 1956 Att 10,203 W 3-2 Scorers: Uphill, Sambrook, Kirk.

v Huddersfield Town Oct 22 1956 Att 9,688 D 3-3 Scorer: Sambrook (3).

v AB Copenhagen (Denmark) Mar 6 1957 Att 5,572 W 1-0 Scorer: Mokone.

v Third Lanark Oct 28 1957 Att 9,018 D 2-2 Scorer: Knox (2). *Inaugural game for new pylon floodlights Preceded by a private practice match. The first of three friendlies to try out the floodlights.*

v Partick Thistle Nov 4 1957 Att 7,539 W 3-2 Scorers: Hill P (2), McPherson. *The second Glasgow side in a week travel south to provide the opposition Roy Kirk scored an own goal.*

v Manchester City Nov 11 1957 Att 8,480 W 3-1 Scorers: Sambrook (2) Knox. *Bert Trautmann played in goal for First Division Manchester.*

v Luton Town Oct 20 1958 Att 6,294 0-0 *Fourth Division City played well against First Division Luton who had no less than five internationals in their side.*

v Sunderland Oct 27 1958 Att 4,979 L 1-3 Scorer: Hill B.

v Banik Ostrava (Czechoslovakia) Sep 24 1959 Att 9,350 L 2-4 Scorers: Ryan, Farmer.

v Slovan Bratislava (Czechoslovakia) Jan 29 1962 Att 8,044 W 2-1 Scorers; Dwight, McCann. *Later the same year Jan Popluhar the Slovan captain played for Czechoslovakia in the World Cup Final in Chile. Brazil won 3-1.*

v TSV Aachen (W Germany) Feb 19 1962 Att 7,100 W 5-3 Scorers: Satchwell (3) ,Dwight, og.

v Luton Town Oct 20 1962 Att 2,670 W 2-1 Scorers; Bly, Dwight.

v Kaiserslautern (W Germany) Nov 26 1963 Att 7,416 W 8-0 Scorers: Humphries, Farmer, Barr, Rees, Hudson (3), Hale. *Unusually City played at home in their all-red change kit.*

v Ferencvaros (Hungary) Dec 16 1963 Att 12,163 W 3-1 Scorers: Hudson, Hale, Mitten. *This was City's tenth consecutive win against foreign opposition.*

v Leicester City Jan 24 1964 Att 13,560 L 0-1. *With both sides making an early exit from the FA Cup this friendly filled the gap. The Sky Blues were Third Division leaders but couldn't find a way past the First Division visitors who had Gordon Banks in goal.*

v Greenock Morton Oct 20 1964 Att 17,029 D 2-2. Scorers: Mitten, Hudson. *"The Enterprise Cup" 1st leg. Bill Glazier made his home debut in goal See: Interesting Away Games for 2nd leg and agg score.*

v Stoke City Oct 1 1965 Att 8,180 W 5-1 Scorers: Hudson (2), Harris, Hill B, Denton. *Second Division Coventry give First Division Stoke, including Dennis Viollet and Maurice Setters in their side, a thrashing.*

v FC Biel (Switzerland) Oct 18 1965 (Cancelled). *The Swiss team despite coming from the hometown of Rolex Omega and Swatch displayed poor timekeeping by pulling out at the last minute Angry Coventry reported the matter to FIFA It is not known if the Swiss-based world body took action.*

v Manchester City Oct 18 1965 Att 5,757 W 4-2. Scorers: Hale (2) Gould, Clements. *Manchester City step in at short notice following Biel's withdrawal.*

v Stade Français (France) Nov 23 1965 Att 3,042 W 4-1. Scorers: Hudson (3) og.

v Greenock Morton Nov 29 1966 Att 4,098 W 3-2. Scorers: Rees, Shepherd, Gould. *Sixteen-year-old Willie Carr made his senior debut as a substitute.*

v Hibernian Feb 7 1969 (Cancelled). *Called off shortly before kick-off due to a snowstorm.*

v Aberdeen Mar 30 1971 Att 8,001 W 1-0 Scorer: Alderson. *City face the Scottish Cup holders and league leaders It's the fourth mid-season friendly since the New Year following two away games and a testimonial. See: Interesting Away Games:Testimonials Away.*

v Gornik Zabrze (Poland) Nov 29 1971 Att 6,838 L 0-2 *Two Bournemouth players, Ted McDougall and Phil Boyer, made guest appearances for Coventry.*

v Washington Diplomats (USA) Mar 24 1981 Att 2,626 W 5-1 Scorers: Thompson (3), English, Coop. *Ex-Southampton men Trevor Hebberd and Malcolm Waldron were in the Diplomats side. Despite City's comfortable victory, an American style shoot-out was staged after the game. Five players from each side were given five seconds to score starting from 35 yards out. The Americans won 3-2 City scorers were Bodak and Blair. Blair scored with a penalty awarded when he was brought down – an unusual penalty within a shoot-out! The men who missed were Bannister, Gillespie and Thomas.*

v St Mirren Dec 22 1987 Att 5331 D 1-1 Scorer: Phillips *"Anglo-Scottish Challenge" First leg. The second leg was never played See: Sky Blue Heaven Vol 1 Worthless Cups.*

v IFK Gothenburg (Sweden) Mar 22 1996. *A behind-closed-doors "warm-up" match on a Friday afternoon. A*

v **Bayern Munich** (Germany) Jan 27 1998 Att 8,409. L 2-4 Scorers: Moldovan, Haworth. *The Bayern side included Kahn, Matthaus, Lizarazu and Basler.*
v **KRC Genk** (Belgium) Aug 30 2000 Att 3,406. W 1-0 Scorer: Roussel. *A pre-season type friendly but after the season had started.*
v **Pakistan** Mar 25 2001 W 2-0. Scorers: Thompson, Aloisi.

END-OF-SEASON HOME FRIENDLIES

v **Burnley** May 10 1962 Att 7,416 L 2-4. Scorers: Byrne, Humphries. *A match to celebrate the consecration of Coventry Cathedral. Johnny Byrne, West Ham's new £60,000 signing from Crystal Palace, was a guest player for City and scored a goal.*
v **Tottenham Hotspur** Apr 28 1964 Att 15,638 L 5-6 Scorers: Hudson (2), Farmer, Kirby, Newton. *Coventry play "Five in Five" (see below).*
v **America FC** (Brazil) Apr 30 1964 Att 10188 L 2-5 Scorer: Hudson (2). *Coventry play "Five in Five". Having won the Third Division Championship on Saturday Apr 25th, the Sky Blues played five friendlies in five days. They flew to Dublin on Monday Apr 27th to play a combined Dublin XI. On Tuesday they played Spurs at home then on Wednesday they took a team to play at Bedworth. Match four is this game on Thursday against America. On Friday they played Eastbourne away in a Benefit match . For details of the away friendlies that week see: Friendlies Away End-of-Season.*
v **Tottenham Hotspur** Apr 29 1965 Att 13680 L 0-3. For Testimonials At Home see: Sky Blue Heaven Vol One.

INTERNATIONAL GAMES STAGED AT HIGHFIELD ROAD

1962 Youth England v Switzerland Nov 22 Att 3,200. Score 1-0 (Jones). *Abandoned after nine minutes – fog.*
1964 U-23 England v Romania Nov 25 Att 2,7476 5-0 Team: Glazier, Badger, Thomson, H Newton, Mobley, Hunter, Murray, Tambling, (Chivers), M Jones, Ball, Hinton. Scorers: Jones, Murray, Ball, Hinton, Chivers. *Coventry City goalie Bill Glazier won his first cap.*
1969 U-23 England v Portugal April 16 Att 13,631.

3-0 Team: Shilton, W Smith, Pardoe, Doyle, Booth, Sadler, Coates, Robson, Clarke, Evans, Sissons. Scorers: Clarke(2), Robson.*Match switched to Highfield Road at late notice after Leicester pulled out.*
1970 Inter-League: Football League v Scottish League March 18 Att 26,693 3-2. Football League: Stepney (Glazier), W Smith, Hughes, Newton, McFarland, Todd, Coates, Kidd, (Peters), Astle, Harvey, Rogers. Scorers: Astle (2), Rogers. Scottish League: McRae, Callaghan, Dickson, Smith, McKinnon, Stanton, McLean, Greig, Hall, (Graham), Cormack, Johnson. Scorers: Cormack, Graham. *The game marked City's 50 years as a League Club Coventry City goalie Bill Glazier was a second half sub for Stepney.*
1973 World Cup: Northern Ireland v Portugal March 28 Att 11,273 1-1 NI: Jennings, O'Kane, Nelson, Neill, Hunter, Clements, Hamilton, Coyle, Morgan, Dickson, O'Neill. Scorers: O'Neill, Eusebio, (Pen). *Coventry City man Dave Clements was in the NI team. Eusebio played for Portugal.*
1980 U-21 England v Scotland European Nations Championship Quarter-Final (1st leg) Feb12 Att 15,382 2-1 England: Bailey, Wright, Sansom, Robson, Osman, Butcher, Hilaire, Hoddle, Crooks, Owen, Rix. Scorers: Owen, Robson. Scotland: Thomson, Stewart, Daeson, Orr, McLeish, Gillespie, Wark, Blair, Archibald, Aitken, Brazil. Scorer: Archibald. *Coventry City players Andy Blair and Gary Gillespie played for Scotland.*
1980 Youth England v Denmark March 26 Att: 2,425 4-0 Team: Kendall (Horn), Bennett, Barnes, Peake, Mabbutt, Pates, Gibson, (Barham), Allen, Hateley, English, MacKenzie. Scorer: Hateley (4). *Trevor Peake and Gary Mabbutt FA Cup Final opponents in 1987 were team mates in this game as were Coventry strikers Mark Hateley and Tommy English.*
1982 Youth England v Scotland European Championships Qual Tie (2nd leg) March 23 Att 2,295 2-2. Scorers: (Eng) Pearson, Walters; (Sco) McStay, Dobbin. England: Francis, Parker, Pickering, Duffield, Elliott, Robson, Singleton, Steven, (Bell), Pearson, Walters, Childs. Scotland: Gunn, McInally, Beaumont, Cooper, Philliben, Black K, McStay, Dobbin, McGivern, Black E, Bowman. *Having won the first leg at Ibrox 1-0 Scotland won 3-2 on aggregate to reach the Finals in*

Finland. John Hendrie of Coventry was injured and missed the chance to play for Scotland but City's Martin Singleton played for England. Two future Sky Blues Nick Pickering and Stewart Robson were also in the England side. Future Coventry City manager Eric Black played for Scotland.

1988 U-21 England v Sweden October 18 Att 3,988 1-1 England: Martyn, B Statham (Burrows), Cooper Sedgley, Redmond, Chettle, White, Ripley, Dozell, (Oldfield), Samways, D Smith. Scorer: White. Sweden: L Eriksson, Nilsson, J Eriksson, Aattovaara, Kamark, Karlsson, Ingesson, Schwartz, J Jansson, Dahlin (Eklund), Andersson. Scorer: Ingesson. *Coventry players Steve Sedgley and David Smith played along with future City player David Burrows.*

OTHER INTERNATIONAL & REPRESENTATIVE MATCHES STAGED AT HIGHFIELD ROAD

1916 Rest of England v Midlands British Red Cross Society Feb 5 Att 8,000. 4-2 Scorers: (Eng) Mercer 2, Hampton, Jones L; (Mids) Jones F Whittingham. A wartime charity match Many players were absent in the war and no Coventry City players were involved although three ex-players including J Pennington of West Bromwich Albion were in the Midlands XI

1945 FA XI v The RAF War Charities Jan 20 Att 13,000 4-6 Scorers: (FA) Lawton (2), Shackleton (2); (RAF) Mortensen (3), Dodds (2), Smith. Joe Mercer, Len Shackleton, Tommy Lawton, and Stan Mortensen were among the players who appeared. Stanley Matthews missed the game for family reasons.

1948 Schoolboy England v Wales Apr 10 Att 25,199 2-1 Scorers: Burkett (2) Harris.

1951 Amateur England v Republic of Ireland Feb 3 Att 8,067 6-3.

1956 Football League Division 3 South v Division 3 North Nov 8 Att 14,156. 2-1 Scorers: (S) Newsham, Hollis; (N) Johnson. A series of games that ran between 1954 and 1958. Goalkeeper Reg Matthews was the only Coventry player in the South team .City manager Harry Warren was in charge of the South while ex-manager Harry Storer then of Derby County selected the North's line-up.

1961 Schoolboy England v Republic of Ireland Apr 8 Att

9,108 8-0 Scorers: Prosser (4), Dawkins, Sissons, Pardoe, Parker.

1967 Schoolboy England v Wales Apr 22 Att 8,465 3-0 Scorers: Lappage (2), Partridge.

1969 Schoolboy England v Netherlands Apr 5 Att 6110 5-2 Scorers: Guthrie (2) Spinner (2) Goodlass

1974 Amateur England v Scotland Apr 5 Att 1,221 1-1.

1978 Schoolboy England v Scotland Apr 29 1-1 Scorers: (Eng) Tate; (Sco) Sheran.

1982 Schoolboy English Schools FA Trophy Final (2nd Leg) Coventry v Sheffield May 4 1-4.

COVENTRY CITY IN REPRESENTATIVE MATCHES AT HOME

1957 Coventry City v All Star Managers' XI Mar 25 Att 6,036 L 1-2 Scorer: McPherson. Benefit Friendly. The all-star team composed of current and past managers including Bill Shankly (Huddersfield Town) and Jack Rowley (Plymouth.) Rowley scored both the managers' goals.

1962 Coventry City v The Army Feb12 Att 3,373 W 2-1 Scorers: Satchwell, Nicholas. The Sky Blues defeat the British Army. Mick Kearns of Coventry played for the Army. All the Army team were professional footballers doing National Servic.e Lt Col Mitchell the Army selector said it was just the preparation his side needed for their forthcoming games against the Belgian and French Army football teams.

1962 Coventry City v England Youth XI Dec 11 Att 3,448 : W 2-1 Scorers: Barr, Rees. The first ever match between a club side and an England team in public. A genuine men against boys contest!

1964 Coventry City Youth v England Grammar Schools May 22 Played at Butts Stadium.

1964 Coventry City v British Olympic XI Mar 2 Att 4,827 L 0-1. The GB side comprised amateurs from non-league football. Despite this impressive win the Olympic side failed to qualify for the Games later that year in Tokyo when they lost 5-3 on aggregate to Greece.

1968 Coventry City U-19 v England Youth XI Mar 19 L 1-4 Scorers: (Cov) Taylor; (Eng) Duffy, Hoy, Foggon, Evans. Coventry's Graham Paddon played for England against City.

1968 Coventry City U-19 v England Youth XI Nov 19 Att

1,659 L1-2 Scorers (Cov) Gould T; (Eng) Stokes, Latchford. David Icke played in goal for City.

1970 Coventry City U-19 v England Youth XI Nov 24 Att 2,199 : L 0-1 Scorer: Durrell.

SENT OFF

COVENTRY CITY PLAYERS SENT OFF IN HOME GAMES 1961-2005

1961-68 None
1968-69 Maurice Setters v Liverpool Apr 22 D 0-0
1969-71 None
1971-72 Ernie Hunt v Liverpool Nov 20 L 0-2
1972-73 None
1973-74 Jimmy Holmes v Manchester City (League Cup) Dec 19 D 2-2
1974-75 None
1975-76 Donal Murphy v Birmingham City Nov 29 W 3-2
1976-77 Larry Lloyd v Manchester Utd Aug 24 L 0-2
Alan Dugdale v Aston Villa Apr 16 L 2-3
1977-79 None
1979-80 Ian Wallace v Crystal Palace Apr 19 W 2-1
1980-83 None
1983-84 Terry Gibson v Grimsby Town (League Cup) Oct 25 W 2-1
Steve Hunt v Southampton Nov 26 D 0-0
1984-85 Brian Kilcline v Manchester Utd Sep 15 L 0-3
1985-87 None
1987-88 Nick Pickering v Manchester Utd Sep 5 D 0-0
1988-89 None
1989-90 Peter Billing v Wimbledon (ZDS Cup) Nov 29 L 1-3
1990-92 None
1992-93 Mick Quinn v Manchester Utd Apr 12 L 0-1
1993-94 None
1994-95 Paul Cook v Wrexham (League Cup) Oct 5 W 3-2
1995-96 Paul Williams v Wimbledon Nov 25 D 3-3
Richard Shaw v Wimbledon Nov 25 D 3-3
1996-97 Dion Dublin v Sunderland Jan 1 D 2-2
1997-98 Paul Williams v Arsenal Jan 17 D 2-2
1998-99 John Aloisi v Charlton Athletic Mar 6 W 2-1
1999-00 None

2000-01 David Thompson v Middlesbrough Aug 19 L 1-3
Carlton Palmer* v Tottenham H Oct 14 W 2-1
Moustapha Hadji v Derby County Mar 31 W 2-0
2001-02 None
2002-03 Youssef Safri v Crystal Palace Aug 24 W 1-0
Youssef Chippo v Watford Feb 1 L 0-1
Gary McSheffrey v Wimbledon Mar 8 D 2-2
2003-04 Youssef Safri v Walsall Aug 16 D 0-0
2004-05 Ian Bennett v Stoke City Feb 26 D 0-0

COVENTRY CITY PLAYERS SENT OFF IN AWAY GAMES 1961-2005

1961-64 None
1964-65 George Hudson v Huddersfield T Feb 13 L 1-2
1965-67 None
1967-68 Dietmar Bruck v Manchester City Mar 9 L 1-3
1968-70 None
1970-71 Ernie Machin v Newcastle Utd Sep 26 D 0-0
1971-72 Chris Cattlin v Everton Oct 2 W 2-1
1972-74 None
1974-75 Chris Cattlin v West Ham Utd Apr 19 W 2-1
1975-76 None
1976-77 John Beck v Aston Villa Nov 20 D 2-2
1977-79 None
1979-80 Ray Gooding v Derby County Dec 26 W 2-1
1980-81 Ray Gooding v Birmingham City Aug 16 L 1-3
Danny Thomas v Leeds (FA Cup) Jan 3 D 1-1
1981-82 Steve Jacobs v Everton Dec 28 1981 L 2-3
Garry Thompson v Aston Villa Feb 27 L 1-2
1982-83 Danny Thomas v Swansea City Aug 31 L 1-2
Garry Thompson v Norwich City (FA Cup) Feb 2 L 1-2
Steve Jacobs v Brighton Apr 23 L 0-1
1983-84 None
1984-85 Terry Gibson v West Brom Nov 24 L 2-5
1985-88 None
1988-89 Trevor Peake v QPR Dec 3 L 1-2
Gary Bannister v Southampton Dec 26 D 2-2
1989-90 Lloyd McGrath v Charlton Ath Oct 28 D 1-1
David Speedie v Sunderland (League Cup) Jan 17 D 0-0

1990-91 David Speedie v Crystal Palace Dec 1 L 1-2

1991-92 Robert Rosario v Southampton Feb 22 D 0-0
   Lloyd McGrath v Leeds Utd Apr 20 L 0-2

1992-93 None

1993-94 Roy Wegerle v Oldham (League Cup) Oct 26
   L 0-2

1994-95 Mick Quinn v Blackburn Rovers Aug 27 L 0-4
   Gary Gillespie v Leicester City Oct 3 D 2-2
   Steven Pressley v Manchester Utd Jan 3 L 0-2
   Paul Cook v West Brom (FA Cup) Jan 18 W 2-1

1995-96 Steve Ogrizovic v Wolverhampton W (League
   Cup) Nov 29 L 1-2
   Kevin Richardson v Aston Villa Dec 16 L 1-4
   David Busst v Plymouth Argyle (FA Cup) Jan 6
   W 3-1

1996-97 Liam Daish v Chelsea Aug 24 L 0-2
   Liam Daish v Birmingham City (League Cup)
   Sep 24 W 1-0
   Noel Whelan v Leeds Utd Dec 26 W 3-1
   Dion Dublin v Blackburn Rovers Jan 11 L 0-4
   Brian Borrows v Newcastle (sub) Mar 15 L 0-4

1997-98 Dion Dublin v Blackburn Rovers Sep 28 D 0-0
   Paul Williams v Aston Villa Dec 6 L 0-3
   Gary Breen v Aston Villa Dec 6 L 0-3
   George Boateng v West Ham Utd Dec 26 L 0-1

1998-99 George Boateng v Leicester City (FA Cup) Jan
   23 W 3-0

1999-00 David Burrows v Leicester City Aug 11 L 0-1
   Youssef Chippo v Sunderland Aug 29 D 1-1
   David Burrows v Tranmere Rovers (League
   Cup) Sep14 1999 L 1-5

2000-01 Paul Williams v Preston NE (League Cup) Sep
   19 W 3-1
   Chris Kirkland v Chelsea Oct 21 L 1-6

2001-02 Lee Hughes v Bradford City Aug 24 L 1-2
   Youssef Safri v Gillingham Sep 29 W 2-1
   David Thompson v Millwall Nov 3 L 2-3
   Marc Edworthy v West Brom Dec 12 L 0-1
   Lee Hughes v Grimsby Town Dec 26 W 1-0
   David Thompson v Wolves Jan 13 L 1-3
   Jay Bothroyd v Crystal Palace Jan 29 W 3-1

2002-03 Calum Davenport v Brighton Aug 13 D 0-0
   Craig Hignett v Burnley Nov 9 L 1-3
   Dean Gordon v Sheffield Utd Dec 28 D 0-0
   Gary Caldwell v Nottingham F Jan 18 D 1-1

2003-04 Patrick Suffo v Preston North End Sep 16 L 2-4
   Michael Doyle v Preston NE Sep 16 L 2-4
   Calum Davenport v Colchester Utd (FA Cup)
   Feb 3 L1-3
   Peter Clarke v Cardiff City Mar 2 W 1-0

2004-05 Louis Carey v Leeds Utd Sep 11 2004 L 0-3
   Steve Staunton v Wigan Athletic Oct 23 L 1-4

BIBLIOGRAPHY

Henderson, Derek	The Sky Blues – The Story of Coventry City Football Club	Stanley Paul 1968
Henderson, Derek	The Coventry City Football Book	Stanley Paul 1970
Foulger, Neville	Coventry: The Complete History of the Club	Wensum 1979
Bailey, Philip; Thorn, Philip and Wynne-Thomas, Peter	Who's Who of Cricketers	Newnes Books 1984
Brassington, David	Singers to Sky Blues The Story of Coventry City Football Club	Sporting & Leisure Press 1986
Dean, Rod	Coventry City – The Complete Record 1883-1991	Breedon Books 1991
O'Connor, Martin and Paul	Coventry City Footballers 1908-1993 The Complete Who's Who	Yore Publications 1993
Edwards, Leigh	The Official Centenary History of the Southern League	Paper Plane 1994
Hill, Jimmy	The Jimmy Hill Story – My Autobiography	Hodder & Stoughton 1998
Brown, Jim	Coventry City The Elite Era – A Complete Record	Desert Island, 1998/2001
Brown, Jim	Coventry City – An Illustrated History	Desert Island, 2000
St. John, Ian	The Saint. My Autobiography.	Hodder & Stoughton, 2005

SUGGESTED READING

Butcher, Terry	Butcher-My Autobiography *with Bob Harris*	Highdown 2005
Imlach, Gary	My Father & Other Working Class Heroes	Yellow Jersey 2005
Gekoski, Rick	Staying Up – A Fan Behind the Scenes in the Premiership	Little, Brown, 1998
Regis, Cyrille	Smoking Joe The Cyrille Regis Story	Spotlite, 2002
Roberts, Brian	Harry's Game	Paper Plane, 1991.
Rowland, George	Coventry City 100 Greatest Footballers	Tempus 2001
Strange, Jonathan	Coventry City A History In 50 Matches	Tempus 2004
Westcott, Chris	Joker in the Pack - The Ernie Hunt Story	Tempus, 2004
Yorath, Terry	Hard Man, Hard Knocks *with Grahame Lloyd*	Celluloid, 2004.

ADDENDUM:
SCORED ON DEBUT
Robbie Keane (2 goals) v Derby Co
Aug 21 1999 W 2-0
Lee Hughes v Stockport Co
Aug 11 2001 W 2-0